Praise for *Cats in th*

'The most enchanting cat book ever'
**Jilly Cooper**

'If you read *Cats in the Belfry* the first time round, be prepared
to be enchanted all over again. If you haven't, then expect to
laugh out loud, shed a few tears and be totally captivated by
Doreen's stories of her playful and often naughty Siamese
cats'
***Your Cat* magazine**

'A funny and poignant reflection of life with a Siamese, that
is full of cheer'
***The Good Book Guide***

Praise for *Cats in May*

'If you loved Doreen Tovey's *Cats in the Belfry* you won't
want to miss the sequel, *Cats in May*… This witty and stylish
tale will have animal lovers giggling to the very last page'
***Your Cat* magazine**

THE COMING OF SASKA

Michael Joseph edition published 1977

This edition published by Summersdale Publishers Ltd. in 2007

Summersdale Publishers Ltd
46 West Street
Chichester
West Sussex
PO19 1RP
UK

www.summersdale.com

Printed and bound in Great Britain.

ISBN: 1-84024-595-6
ISBN 13: 978-1-84024-595-0

4

# THE
# COMING OF
# SASKA

## DOREEN TOVEY

summersdale

## Also by Doreen Tovey

# One

WHEN I TOLD FATHER Adams we were planning another trip to the Rockies – to do some more riding, I said, and look for the grizzlies we'd missed last time, and if possible see something of the wolves – he looked at me as if I needed certifying.

He usually does look at me like that, of course. Charles and I have lived along the lane from him for more than eighteen years now, but in his eyes we are still essentially townsfolk and therefore dim beyond redemption when it comes to the commonsense matters of life.

This time, however, he regarded me even more old-fashionedly than usual. 'Hassn't thee got enough wild animals round here?' he said. And then, in a voice deep with concern because really he is rather fond of us, 'Thee'st want to watch thee dussn't get *et*.'

I knew what he was thinking of. For one thing the previous week, when we'd been bringing down logs from our two and a half acres of woodland, which is across the lane from the cottage. It could almost have been a scene from the Canadian backwoods then, with Charles stacking the logs at the road-edge and me loading them on to a roughly constructed sledge so that Annabel, our donkey, could haul them down to the cottage.

The idea of the sledge was because the hill is so steep. With wheels the load of logs would probably have shot straight to the bottom with Annabel on top – but with runners it slid gently down behind her, the weight acting as a brake, and it towed up easily again when empty.

Annabel loved it. Not wanting to over-burden her... she is, after all, only a very small donkey... at first I'd tied just a couple of logs to the sledge. She'd wafted them down to the valley as if they were balloons, so next time I'd added a couple more... and the time after that another two... until eventually she was pulling quite a load on every trip. Enjoying it, too. Plodding down the hill with the air of an experienced, if pint-sized, dray-horse and the complacently smug expression on her face that Charles and I knew only too well.

She stood patiently at the bottom while I unloaded the logs on to the grass verge outside the cottage; pulled the sledge back up again without even the slightest pause (normally I'd have to haul her up it bodily, with her fighting to eat dandelions at every step); stood again at the top while I re-loaded... 'I wish we had a camera handy,' I said to Charles as, with me walking at her head, she started down the hill once more. 'Or that somebody would come along and see her. Nobody ever *does* when she's being good like this.'

That did it. Mention the word 'good' in Annabel's hearing and, it being her lifelong principle to be the opposite, non-co-operation sets in at the speed of sound. At the end of that descent she decided she'd had enough of playing at draught horses. Unfortunately I had my foot on the sledge-rope at the time, anchoring it while I unloaded the logs, so when she moved off down the other fork of the lane (away, that is, from any direction that could possibly be connected with log-hauling), she not only took the still half-loaded sledge with her but me as well, sliding along behind it on my bottom with my foot caught in the rope.

Overburden her, did I say? The sledge and I went down the lane behind her as if we were so much balsa wood. The lane leads, if one follows it far enough, to the field of a donkey friend of hers called Charlie, some three miles away, and I'd no doubt have gone the whole way to Charlie's on my seat if it hadn't been that Father Adams happened to be a short way down there clearing a blockage in the stream at the time, and Annabel shied and stopped when she saw his head come up out of the ditch.

I scrambled up, grabbed her bridle and explained what had happened. Father Adams said nothing for a moment. Just looked at me resignedly from under his hat brim. 'Wur's the Boss?' he asked at length. When I explained that Charles was still up at the top of the hill bringing logs out to the road-edge... I *had* shouted but he couldn't have heard me above the noise of the stream, I said, and anyway he was singing when I left... that didn't help things either. Charles has a very good voice but his habit of singing when working among his fruit trees is down on Father Adams's scorecard as another of our peculiarities.

I remember on one occasion Charles rendering 'On Yonder Hill Declining' from *Fra Diavolo*... standing on a slope in the orchard, one arm out-thrown in the manner of Gigli, performing, as he thought, entirely for my benefit...

and in the pause after a ringing 'Dia... vo... lo... o prou...
oud... ly stands' a familiar voice floated up from the lane,
'Ah, an' if he done a bit more weedin' instead of standin',
maybe we could see the trees for the nettles.'

No. Years of being our nearest neighbour and therefore
rarely missing a thing we do has done nothing to alter
Father Adams's conviction that what we need is a keeper. If
I couldn't cope with a donkey hauling logs, I could see him
thinking, what chance would I have against a grizzly?

We couldn't even win with Siamese cats. We had two.
Seeley, a four-year-old Seal Point and Shebalu, a two-
year-old Blue Point. And if evidence was needed of our
ineptitude in that direction there was, to take the latest
example, the affair of Seeley and the dog-food.

This had come about as the result of the husband of
Shebalu's breeder calling to see us one day when he was
on business in our neighbourhood. 'Good Lord, hasn't she
grown!' he said, hardly able to believe that the tall, beautiful,
serenely elegant Blue Point who swayed top-model fashion
across the room to greet him was the same matchstick-tailed
little scrap who used to race up and down his curtains. 'She's
twice the size of her mother.'

'It's the country air,' I told him. 'And tearing about the
hillside. And of course she eats like a horse.' At which we
got to talking about feeding – pigs' hearts and lean mince
they liked, I said, and didn't it cost a bomb... tinned food
was good and cheaper, but we couldn't get them to eat much
of it... and he said Shebalu's mother didn't like tinned cat-
food either, but now they fed her on Chum. She and their
dog side by side, from twin bowls, and she ate it as though
it were caviare.

Aha! I thought. The next time I went to the village shop I too brought home some Chum. Shebalu was the real stumbling block when it came to the tinned cat-food business. Seeley, our amiable gannet, would eat it if he had to. It was just that it didn't seem fair to feed him on tinned stuff while Shebalu held out for fresh meat. If her mother liked dog-food, however, perhaps she would, too, and that would solve the problem. Not only as regards cost. Our Vet had told us years before that cats *should* eat a fair proportion of tinned pet food. It was scientifically balanced, he said – particularly the kind that contained cereal – and cats were much less likely to get kidney trouble in later life if their diet wasn't exclusively meat and fish.

So I got the Chum. Shebalu refused to look at it, saying she didn't care what her mother said. What jurisdiction did She have, anyway, letting her Daughter leave home at Eight Weeks Old, bawled Abandoned Annie indignantly at the very thought of it. Seeley tunnelled into it saying it was super... better than rabbit, he assured us between noisily appreciative slurps. How were we to know that, having eaten his and Shebalu's platefuls and presumably seen the picture on the tin, his Siamese mind would translate that into meaning that *he* was now a dog, so from now on he was going to behave like one?

He started that very afternoon. When I opened the back door to take them out for their four o'clock run, there, on the other side of it, was one of our neighbours about to put the church news-sheet through our letterbox. Behind her was her dog, a huge black muscle-rippling Labrador at the sight of whom Seeley would normally have fled indoors and hidden under the table.

What, fortified by Chum, did he do on this occasion? Stick his neck out, growl like a guard dog, and charge. 'Seeley!' I screeched, diving after him. 'Bramble!' yelled the woman, making a futile grab at her dog. Round the corner of the cottage we tore, expecting to find Seeley demolished on the lawn – and what incredible scene met our eyes?

Bramble sitting down hard on the front path, presumably to stop himself from running away, shivering like a jelly with his ears flat in surrender... and, stalking intimidatingly towards him like Gary Cooper in *High Noon*, our normally timid little Seeley.

I grabbed him, wondering what he might do to me in that mood, but he knew even then that I was his friend. He let me carry him away, his coat bushed out like a porcupine, contenting himself with shouting threats over my shoulder as he went. Show his nose in our Valley again and he'd have his Ears off, he bawled at the terrified Bramble. Set foot on our Path and he'd Eat Him. Wet Just Once More on our gatepost and he'd... what dreadful Siamese retribution that would incur we didn't hear. By that time I'd dumped him in the conservatory and locked the door.

I apologised to our neighbour saying it must have been the dog-food and she said she reckoned the Rector should pay her danger money... both of us laughing, seeing that nobody had been hurt, and neither of us serious in what we said... and a week later Seeley did it again.

This time he'd been up on the hillside in the Forestry Commission estate with me and Shebalu. Basking in the late afternoon sunshine, hunting in the bracken for mice, the pair of them chasing each other up the fir trees... Shebalu shinning effortlessly up like a stevedore mounting the Eiffel Tower; Seeley, like Solomon before him, achieving four feet up with an excited yell to Look At Him and then falling off with a plop. They'd had their fun and were back sitting on the rug with me when a man leading a horse and accompanied by a boy and an Alsatian dog appeared in the lane below us.

Normally – this, for safety's sake, was something I'd taught them long ago – when we saw a dog the three of us vanished silently into the undergrowth. A right nit I felt too, at times, crouched in a clump of bracken peering out with a couple of cats, but I thought it was good to set an example.

This time, however, before I could make a move, Seeley was up and streaking downhill to the attack. True when he reached the bottom and the Alsatian barked at him he lost his nerve and dodged into an old stone ruin; just over the Forestry fence, it had always been a refuge for our cats. But no sooner did the bitch turn away, called off by the man who said she wouldn't harm him, she was young and only playing, than Seeley shot out again like a cannon ball, thinking her retreat meant that she was afraid of *him*.

By this time, actually, she was. Back to her owner she fled, with Seeley like an avenging fury at her heels. Up in the air went the horse – thank goodness the man wasn't riding him. How I managed to field Seeley as he passed me I will never know. Only that somehow, as in a dream, I did – reflex action is second nature to the owners of Siamese cats – and that I was dimly aware in the background of the man hanging on to the rearing horse, the boy getting up on the bank for safety, Charles running like mad down from the orchard – and, watching from the lower lane, registered even in my extremis by the downturned brim of his trilby, the silent. Job-like figure of Father Adams.

Sometimes I wonder how he does it. Fell a tree up in the top hedge of our wood and round the corner as it falls will come Father Adams. Not deliberately, because he's heard the sawing and wants to know who it is, but because he's happened to come that way home from the pub. Get out quietly repairing one of our garden walls – they are dry-stone walls and always tumbling down – and, just as one puts on a wrongly-balanced stone and the whole lot falls down again, there on the other side of it will be Father Adams.

It was a foregone conclusion, therefore, that he'd be in at the end of the dog-food experiment. It was a few days later and we'd stopped giving Seeley Chum. Another Siamese owner had told us that her Vet said one shouldn't feed cats on dog-food. Different types of animals have different metabolisms, she said, and the foods are geared specially to their needs.

We did rather wonder – while telling ourselves that the dog-chasing was, of course, just coincidence – whether leaving it off would make a difference in that respect. Even we didn't bargain for anything so spectacular, however, as that on Wednesday there was Seeley chasing an Alsatian and by Sunday, sans the Chum, we were back to dogs chasing *him*.

'Whass he doin' up there?' asked Father Adams, appearing as if by press-button as we once more hoisted our extension ladder against an ash-tree some fifty yards down the lane. Down through the leaves, from the top-most branch, peered two blue eyes round with woe. Like Solomon before him, while normally a non-climber, when danger threatened he could get up all right; the snag was, also like Solomon, that he then developed vertigo and couldn't get down.

'Don't tell I he've chased a dog up *there*,' went on Father Adams, ready after eighteen years to believe anything as far as our animals were concerned. Anything, that is, except the truth. That Seeley had fled up there at the sight of a passing Corgi and didn't Father Adams think it queer, I said, that he'd chased dogs when we gave him dog-food and got chased by them when we didn't?

'Sometimes it strikes I thee bist,' said our neighbour, who is a man of few but succinct words. In the circumstances it was hardly surprising that he worried about us meeting up with grizzlies.

# Two

NORMALLY MISS WELLINGTON WOULD have worried too. She was always worrying about other people. Whether somebody ought to be told about the way they kept their garden. (Miss Wellington's, where it could be seen for the stone gnomes and toadstools that dotted it like the Bayeux Tapestry, was immaculate and couldn't be faulted.) Whether Annabel was happy. Miss Wellington spent many an anxious hour pondering this at Annabel's fence and, because Annabel always bawled when she moved away, was sure she needed a companion. Annabel was actually informing the world that Miss Wellington was stingy with the peppermints... we could always tell her disgusted calls by the derisive snort at the end. But Miss Wellington liked to worry. It made life so much more interesting.

She worried about the church heating. She worried about what things were coming to. She worried considerably about the young people of today. She'd done that ever since she saw their goings on on television and now – which was why she wasn't as yet at hysteria stations at the thought of us going out to look for grizzlies – she had a trendy young couple living next door to her and she was worrying more than ever.

Convinced that all young men with beards had sinister motives and that flowing dresses and beads were a sign of fecklessness in girls, Miss Wellington nearly dropped when she saw the Bannetts looking over Rose Cottage. Ern Biggs, Father Adams's rival for the handyman jobs in the village, was working in a nearby garden at the time and according to him she went straight indoors and started playing hymns on her piano. 'Oh God Our Help In Ages Past,' he said, and whether it was to frighten them off or in the hope of invoking heavenly protection nobody knew, but either way it didn't work. The Bannetts bought the cottage, Miss Wellington fluttered round the village anticipating the worst – the place taken over by hippies and probably a pop festival on the village green before we'd finished... and the week before they moved in, everybody had a fright.

Everybody except us, that is. We happened to be coming back from town around ten o'clock at night and while, as we turned the corner by the Rose and Crown and drove along the lane, we were startled ourselves for a moment to see Rose Cottage apparently floodlit, with music throbbing out from it like Congo drums, we did get the true picture as we passed.

The Bannetts were showing another couple around (Liz Bannett's parents, it later transpired). The son et lumière effect was the result of their having switched on the high-powered lamps installed by the builders for working on the dark, low-ceilinged interior. During the day, when the builders were using them, the lights didn't show up so much; at night, through the uncurtained windows, they shone out like the Eddystone lighthouse. The music, we further realised as we drove slowly past with the car windows down (being as interested in our neighbours as anybody), was Beethoven... probably there was a concert on the radio... and it could be heard so clearly because the cottage door was open: the Bannetts and their visitors were just leaving and Tim Bannett was turning off the lights.

That wasn't how the story hit the village, though. 'Wunt half a party up at Rose Cottage last night,' Father Adams told us when he brought us in some leeks. 'Place all lit up like a gin palace,' said Fred Ferry when I met him in the lane. The Rose and Crown was the nearest he'd ever been to a gin palace but Fred likes a dramatic turn of phrase. 'People up there drinkin' and carryin' on,' Ern informed everybody he met. This was his interpretation of Fred's gin palace, of course. Ern lives in the next village himself and hadn't personally witnessed anything.

If Miss Wellington had heard the Beethoven she might have been happier about her prospective neighbours. Miss Wellington is a great believer in culture. But she happened to be away visiting her brother for a couple of days and was told the tale, on her return, by Father Adams. Supported by Fred Ferry and Ern Biggs, of course, who were at her gate as fast as their boots would carry them. We were very kind, she told us when we tried to give her our version of the affair. She realised we were trying to spare her. She knew as well as we did what modern young people were like, however. She'd never be surprised at anything that happened.

Miss Wellington was always expecting things to happen. Only recently one of our neighbours had had his car banged in the lane near the church, by somebody coming round the corner on the wrong side. Miss Wellington's comment on this had been that it wasn't safe to go out these days without taking a bath and when I asked what that had to do with it – 'In case one were hurt and taken to hospital,' said Miss W. 'One wouldn't want to go there dirty, would one?'

What with presumably taking baths and waiting for the next-door orgies to start. Miss Wellington was pretty busy that summer. She was conspicuous by her absence from the preparations for our safari, anyway, which was probably just as well. It would only have needed her at her usual rate of attendance and we'd have gone clean up the wall.

There was so much to do, and so many people to tell us how to do it. For a start there was the garage door to be repaired. One of a pair of doors actually, made of heavy metal sheeting on wooden frames, and over the years one of the doorposts had rotted, and the door on that side had sagged and was dragged nightly into position by Charles with a horrible shrieking noise, and Father Adams had been saying for months that if we didn't put he right we'd have a fine old job on there, and now of course we had. Not only was the door off its hinges at the top, but with all the dragging, the metal sheeting was adrift from its frame, bent into the bargain, and Charles was saying we couldn't go to Canada and leave the door like that.

I couldn't see why not. We left it like that every time we went out, propped up with a spade so it wouldn't fall down, and nobody had tampered with it yet. It contained, in any case, only our old car, our 16-foot canoe (either of which would have been spotted by the neighbours to a man if it had gone up the hill with anybody else) and a load of old junk that nobody but Charles could find a use for. Even he, I sometimes doubted, would hardly find a use for the picture of his Aunt Ethel as a girl clutching a tennis racket, or a step-ladder minus its steps.

Charles thought otherwise, however, so there he was for about a fortnight, putting in a new doorpost, hammering the metal sheeting flat, making a complete new frame for the back of the door... every morning laying the whole thing on the driveway for easy working and every night hoisting it back to fill the gap again.

Our mentors were in their element, of course. 'Told thee theest should have done he months ago,' Father Adams advised us a dozen times a day. 'Still working' on thee raft then?' was Fred Ferry's daily quip about how we were going to Canada. 'Theest do better to let I finish he,' Ern Biggs said hopefully and persistently – to which Father Adams's reply was that finished it certainly would be if Ern Biggs ever laid hammer to it.

Finished it eventually was, though – perfectly, as Charles does everything, though it takes him a time in the doing of it. And then he painted it, still flat on the drive for convenience and, as the paint wasn't dry, for the first time ever we didn't hoist it into the gap that night and the next morning we found we had visitors.

We'd noticed them the previous evening. Two exhausted swallows resting on our telephone wire after their thousand-mile flight from Africa: a sign that summer had come. 'Young ones,' said Charles. 'Probably born up at the farm last year.' And then, after marvelling at the tremendous distance they'd flown and the instinct that brought them back to raise their own young in this remote corner of England where they themselves had been born, we thought no more about it. They were just resting. They wouldn't stay with us. We'd never had swallows in the Valley. At the farm at the top of the hill, yes – they'd nested in the barn up there for years. But the only comparable structure in the Valley was Annabel's stable and obviously the roof of that wasn't high enough for them.

Except that now there was our garage with its door off, on the very evening the swallows arrived... and there was this young pair (they reminded him of the Bannetts, said Charles) obviously wanting to set up on their own... though how they could have known our garage door was off, nearly half a mile away from the barn...

They were still there next morning, perched on the wire, considering the space where the door should have been and occasionally venturing through it. They watched everything that happened during the day. The cats going up to the vegetable garden to eat grass, Annabel being led out of her stable and put up on the hill, Charles putting a second coat of paint on the recumbent door... careful to avoid appearing to notice them but they were certainly studying him, he said. Several times the male had swooped daringly low over his head while the female, much more cautious, twittered anxiously, like Miss Wellington, from the wire.

They moved in, of course. Who wouldn't with those high rafters waiting to be nested in, mud for building in the stream bank by the garden wall, a valley full of insects for the catching and a couple of humans who, having been deliberately tested, obviously didn't object to swallows?

There was no question of our putting back the garage door. There it stood, propped against the wall, while Father Adams said we were never right, Fred Ferry told everybody we couldn't rehang it because it didn't fit, and the swallows swept confidently in and out. 'What be goin' to do when theest go to Canada?' asked Ern. Charles said the brood would be flying by then.

They were flying all right. We watched through the weeks – when we should have been doing so many other things – while the nest was built, like a tiny parson's pulpit, high under the roof, snug against a rafter: while the eggs were laid, and then hatched – there were four of them – and the cleverness of the nesting site was revealed. They'd chosen the one rafter that adjoined a bracing strut that ran right across the garage and there, when they were hatched, four little swallows were able to sidle out, even before they could fly, sit in a row as on a trapeze bar, and peer out at what went on in the garden. What was more, said Charles, if they did fall they'd land in the canoe, which was suspended by ropes from the roof. Wasn't that clever of the parents?

It certainly was, though we didn't appreciate it quite so much when we got the canoe down one afternoon to do a bit of practice on the river and saw what they'd done to the inside. Four little swallows sitting up there getting excited... still, as Charles said, at least it kept it off the car.

Where, you may ask, were the cats while all this was going on? In the canoe themselves, if they got the chance. They would get on the car roof, from there up into the canoe, and sit there one in each seat section. They couldn't reach the swallows, who knew it perfectly well and took no notice of them. We didn't bother either – for once we knew where the pair of them were – but it certainly shook Ern Biggs when he saw them. He'd called to ask if we wanted any work done. I sent him up to see Charles, who was in the garage, and he'd looked up when he heard the swallows twittering. 'N there were thic cats,' he reported later in the Rose and Crown, 'sittin' up in thic canoe, like a couple of they Polynesian Islanders.' He'd apparently added that, knowing us, it wouldn't have surprised he if they'd paddled the ruddy thing out of the garage.

We soldiered on. We couldn't put the door back but there were plenty of other things to be done. Getting the garden straight; studying maps and getting our luggage together; me practising up on my riding.

For me this was a necessity. Among other things we were going to revisit our friends on a couple of Alberta ranches and while I knew full well that Charles, as had happened last time, would go out there not having ridden for ages, leap into a Western saddle and go careering about the range as if he'd been born on it, I also knew that I, who never missed a week without riding in England, didn't have Charles's way with horses whatsoever.

On our last visit I'd been lent, on one ranch, a fat little cow-pony called Sheba who was adept at slipping her saddle. True I'd had to concentrate on riding lop-sidedly – to get her saddle back straight every time she slipped it sideways because I hadn't a clue as to how to tighten a cinch. But that should have been all in a day's work. I shouldn't, as both she and I knew was the case, have been in danger of vanishing over the horizon if for a moment I let her have her head.

This time, I decided, it would be different. I too would manage my horse, like Charles, by the way I sat it and used my legs. I too would ride nonchalantly, reins in one hand, with my mount moving obediently beneath me. To which end I was practising diligently at the local stables, supervised by Mrs Hutchings and her daughter.

As always I rode Mio, the Number Two horse of the remuda. Merlin was still there – 20 years old now, the grand old man of the stables and still the best bet on which to mount beginners: carrying them carefully as babies until he knew they had their balance, then cantering with them regardless – though still gently – just to prove to them that they could go. So was Cobnut, the fast little dark chestnut gelding beloved of my friend Tina, who was a nurse. So were Gusto who, with me clinging to his neck, had once given a Wild West bucking demonstration, and Kelly, the eternally doleful Irish horse, and Alex, the big chestnut hunter.

Of the others. Halberdier was now retired, Zaboine had been bought by his favourite rider and gone to live with him on Exmoor – and Jasper, the tall black thoroughbred, was dead.

Tragedy had struck once more, as it can so easily with thoroughbreds. Jasper had developed leg trouble, which had been diagnosed as chronic arthritis. He'd had supports, injections, lengthy, expensive treatment... Lynn Hutchings, who'd trained him from a yearling, had nursed him like a baby. It was no use. At first there were intervals when his leg appeared to be normal – and then, for no apparent reason, he would be limping, in pain again. If he was kept in his box, his leg improved to a degree but he became bad-tempered with frustration. If he was put out to grass, even on his own, he would try to gallop because that, for him, was what life was for – and his leg would go again. Towards the end, while the Vet tried a last desperate treatment to save him, he lived permanently in his box. It was heartbreaking to see him watching as the other horses went out on a ride. Gusto, who'd been his grazing companion in happier days on the hill. Mio, with whom he'd loved to race. And then Jasper, whose joy it had been to skim across the Downs as if on wings, would come out for his own exercise and limp painfully around the yard.

The treatment failed. There was nothing more to be done, said the Vet... and sadly the Hutchings agreed. There was no question of retiring him like Halberdier. He would have been in pain for the rest of his life. So now Jasper was gone, at only seven years old, and in his place was Kestrel: a fine-tempered chestnut thoroughbred who looked very like Zaboine. There was also, which complicated things considerably, another newcomer called Barbary.

# Three

'YOU'LL LIKE HIM – HE'S just your cup of tea,' said Mrs Hutchings when she told me they'd bought Barbary. What she meant by that I wasn't sure. Mio, to me, was my cup of tea – the horse I would have owned had it been possible. A three-quarter Arab, beautiful, fast, with the gracefully swaying hindquarters of the pedigree. Hindquarters which he'd used on countless occasions to cart me off, gathering them beneath him for his famous leap and we'd be away up the track as if he were Pegasus.

I'd improved mind you. He didn't get away quite so often and when he did I didn't, these days, grab the saddle. ('Pulling leather' they call it on the Western range, where it is regarded as the hallmark of the dude.) No. These days I sat there, hands down, and battled every inch of the way. We went sideways, in circles, up on his hind legs ... it surprised me sometimes to realise I was doing it. 'Splendid,' Mrs Hutchings would call. 'Now let him out gently... make him trot before you canter.' I hadn't got that part of it yet. The moment I let Mio out he went like an arrow with a jet engine attached. But at least I sat the arrow now with a modicum of direction: not with my eyes shut, holding the saddle and praying.

Why then did Mrs Hutchings think I'd like Barbary? He was another one in Mio's class, she said. Fast, eager... easy to control so long as one sat him properly. And it would be good for me to occasionally ride another horse, particularly as we were going out to Canada where I'd probably ride a variety anyway.

I tried Barbary. I didn't think he was like Mio. His trot was jerkier. He didn't leap into a canter. He was fast, admittedly, but he didn't fight control or throw his head about, or gallop with it turned sideways, as Mio did. Mio was better practice for prancing about on the range – besides which, he and I had rapport. If our land at the cottage had been flat enough and if the Hutchings would have parted with him... in spite of what I'd said about never owning horses, Mio would have been living with us.

So I went back to riding Mio and Tina tried out Barbary, and said she didn't like him as much as Nutty either. His trot wasn't so smooth, she said... admittedly he cantered well... but there wasn't that sense of *competition*.

I knew what she meant. Tina had recently achieved a spectacular in which, holding open the gate to the Downs while the rest of the party went through, she'd asked the last rider to wait, not to canter until she herself had come through – and the other rider, taking no notice, had gone belting after the others. Tina, on the wrong side of the wall, had gone up in the air on the excited Nutty and had come down back to front. Thinking she'd then got him under control she'd turned him towards the gate – and up he'd gone again, all four feet in the air, and whirled a complete circle in the opposite direction.

Tina had fallen off. Nutty had bolted through the gate and they'd had quite a job to catch him. It was because he thought he was being left behind, of course. There was nothing vicious about Nutty. But, said Tina, she *shouldn't* have come off. So now she was insisting on opening all the gates, deliberately going through last and making him wait till she was ready. He still whipped round at every gate like a spinning top, but he'd never again managed to unseat her.

That, and trying to hold him when he raced with Mio, was what Tina regarded as competition. Not going along on Barbary, fast though he was, as uneventfully as if he were on tramlines.

For a while that was, and then Barbary began to get his bearings. He hadn't been unfit when he came – it was just that for a while before he was sold he hadn't been used much. Now his muscles were hard and he'd sized up the other horses... he could lick any of that lot, he said. He proceeded to do it every time they took him out, and the excursions became progressively devastating. First it was on the other rides that we heard he'd run away with someone... or stampeded the entire outfit, charging past it from the rear. Then it was on our ride that we would hear a warning yell from Tina and pull over to one side as Barbary came flashing through. He was getting stronger, said Tina... it was practically impossible to hold him. Nonsense, said Mrs Hutchings. Tina didn't sit down hard enough.

I didn't either, of course. That was a well-known fact. So it was hardly surprising, the one time in that period when

I did ride Barbary, that I met with little success. Mio and Nutty were on holiday – all the horses had a fortnight's rest in turn in the summer and the two of them were out at grass together. Tina was away too, on holiday in North Africa, from which she returned quite overcome at having cantered on a camel.

Normally people only trotted on them, it seemed, held on a leading rein by an accompanying camel boy, but she'd explained that she rode in England and asked if they could go fast... and at the exact time that she was careering over the desert on a camel keeping up the reputation of the British for being mad, I, on her darned Barbary, was in danger of breaking my neck.

As was always my downfall, it was on a downward slope. For most of the ride I'd ridden ahead of the group, like Napoleon on his charger. Mrs Hutchings said she'd found it the safest way with people who were likely not to be able to hold him. If he took off when he was in front he wouldn't stampede the rest – in fact when he was in front he usually didn't bother to go. It was just his desire to show he could beat them that sent him zipping past the others.

She was right. Out in front... very much out in front: I had no desire to play a harp... I walked him, trotted, cantered, and wondered what the fuss was about. He certainly was stronger than when I'd first ridden him; even walking one could sense his sprung-steel gait. But even at his fastest he still reacted straight to the bit: I didn't have to fight to stop him, as with Mio.

Until, that was, we were on the homeward run, with the horseshoe bend ahead of us, and Mrs Hutchings, knowing my record on downward slopes, said I'd better take him, now, to the back. If I kept him well into the other horses' tails he couldn't get through if he tried. They'd be walking down it anyway, so there wouldn't be any incentive, and once we were down and round the bend... Well, if he took off then, I knew I could always sit him.

Unfortunately he took off before that. There we were going downhill to the bend, the horses bunched tightly, me at the back. There, on the right of the track, was an open, boulder-strewn plateau simply asking to be run away on. 'Quick! Across here!' snorted Barbary, who'd apparently been watching cowboy films on television. And across there, like escapees from an Indian war-party, we suddenly wheeled and went. Jumping rocks, narrowly missing holes, racing to cut off the others... who by this time, having been set off by Barbary's antics, were going like a posse themselves: sticking to the track, though, with Mrs Hutchings at their head.

'Sit down,' she shrieked across at me, but I couldn't. Not going downhill with Barbary's bouncing gait. I clung, sweating, to his neck. I saw the track reappear beneath his feet. At least we'd missed all the boulders. 'Mind the *edge*,' yelled Mrs Hutchings – and boy, now there was another snag. We'd shot across the track and now we were zooming round the horseshoe on its inside, right on the edge of the dropover.

There was nothing I could do about it. By this time Barbary had bounced my feet out of the stirrups and I could only cling to his neck and hold on. We made it, though, and once round the bend I got my stirrups back and heaved myself upright in the saddle. We went up the track as if the Apaches were after us... but at the end of it we stopped as suddenly as we'd started and waited placidly for the others.

'So endeth that lesson,' said Mrs Hutchings when she came up. 'It's all because you won't sit *down*.' Which wasn't what she said when, shortly afterwards, she too began to have trouble with Barbary.

Whether it was his natural behaviour, coming out now that he was on form. Whether it was that, encouraged by his success with the rest of us, he was determined to complete his record in full. Whether it was that Mrs Hutchings, seeing what he did with us, became temporarily demoralised herself... the fact remained that the time came when she couldn't hold him either and the rider who came belting past from the rear, shouting 'Quick! Out of the way! I'm coming!' was as likely to be her as one of us.

It created an interesting situation. As she said, she wasn't scared of him: she knew she wouldn't come off. But she couldn't very well ride him when she was shepherding children or beginners: it set a bad example to say the least. At the same time she had to try to master him – in competition with the other horses, because it was only under those conditions that he bolted... so when did she do her practice? When Tina and I were with her.

Nowadays there were four of us who usually rode together. Tina, myself, a girl called Penny and her husband Keith. Keith, a good rider, always had Kestrel. Penny, more nervous, generally had Kelly. With us, said Mrs Hutchings, she didn't mind. There were enough of us to block her way if she wanted to try staying at the back. We were competent enough not to chase her if Barbary was out in front. 'Oh yes, you are,' she said, seeing my eyes roll heavenwards. 'You can hold Mio if you try.'

So now we embarked on a series of rides when, instead of Mrs Hutchings shepherding us and giving us encouragement, we solicitously took care of her. 'Wait here, I'm going to try to walk him,' she would say when we got to a stretch where the horses usually cantered, and there we would sit in careful order. Mio and Kestrel in front so that, being fastest, when we did go they wouldn't tangle with the other; Nutty next so that if he did his pirouette and take-off there were two of us ahead to block him (not that Tina minded it by now but we had Mrs H. to think of); Kelly at the rear because, apart from being slowest, he kicked out if any other horse tried to pass him.

And Mrs Hutchings would advance alone, like a knight going out to joust. One step... two... Barbary would start his prancing. 'You're doing fine! You've got him!' we would call encouragingly from behind. And then she'd ease the reins the fraction necessary to allow him to go forward... and there'd be a sudden volcanic eruption and Barbary would be gone.

I got my practice for the prairies, all right. I got it in those vital moments after Barbary took off. When Kestrel, Mio and Nutty wanted to go too and we, to give Mrs Hutchings a breathing space, doggedly fought to hold them.

Kestrel's method of protest was to buck – and never outside of a rodeo have I seen a horse that could buck so high and wide. Keith, hat over his eyes, flew up and down on him. I, on Mio, pranced sideways, backwards and in circles. Nutty, with Tina aboard, cavorted and sidestepped behind us. Once, trying to free himself from the bit, Mio backed into Kestrel as he was bucking. Like a stone from a catapult Mio shot forward, bucking furiously too. 'For goodness sake get going!' shrieked Tina from behind us. 'I can't hold Nutty another second with you two doing that circus act!'

How right she was. The next instant she went past us like Annie Oakley, disappearing up the track in a cloud of dust. Kestrel came down from his buck and took off after Nutty. Kelly, his Irish gloom forgotten for once, came galumphing up from the rear. So far I'd managed to hold Mio – only because I had him back to front, mind you, facing away from the way he wanted to go – but now, with a wrench of his head, he was on his hind legs... he'd turned, he'd done his leap, and we were zooming after the others. 'Like Roy Rogers,' I remember thinking as we spun round in the air, and if only we'd had a cine film of the incident...

A cameraman would have had a field day over our escapades with Barbary. One fast horse perpetually taking off along a track and, a few seconds later, three equally fast ones racing after him. Sometimes, when we caught up with her, Mrs Hutchings would be at the end of the track, with Barbary under control and peacefully grazing: we slowed to a trot before we got there then, not to set him off by charging up to him. Sometimes we misjudged and caught her up halfway and then we all swept along together... Kestrel bucking in protest because for Mrs H.'s sake Keith wouldn't let him pass Barbary, Mio right on Kestrel's heels, jumping sideways in mid-gallop to avoid the bucks... then, finding he was on the grass verge and that the way was clear ahead, deciding now was the time to show the pair of them. 'Come on! Let's go!' he would snort, sticking his head out. And I'd be practically flat on my back in the saddle trying to stop him.

Once we lost Mrs Hutchings in a hill fog. That was actually rather frightening. I can see her now taking off up the track, the mist closing in behind her, and hear the staccato sound of Barbary's hooves fading gradually away in the distance. We waited longer than usual before going after her, so that we wouldn't come on her unawares in the mist and run the risk of collision. For once we were holding the horses without any trouble: they were standing there quietly grazing. Probably the fog had muffled Barbary's hoofbeats even for them, though they hadn't forgotten he was somewhere up in front. The moment we decided to go and touched our heels to their sides, they were away up the track like greyhounds.

We let them go flat out, knowing that Barbary was well ahead. We expected to find him waiting where the track we were on joined another one. We slowed as we approached the spot – but Barbary wasn't there. Probably Mrs Hutchings couldn't stop him and had gone on to the next one, we thought. So we gathered speed again and swept on. Only Barbary wasn't at the next crossing either and the track led on from there straight for the moors. The gate was a quarter of a mile ahead of us, but she wouldn't have gone out through that...

'Not unless he took her over it,' said someone, and we sat there imagining the worst. Barbary damaging himself out on the moors. Mrs Hutchings lying unconscious, our being unable to find her because of the mist... which was so thick now we could hardly see each other, let alone somebody lying on the ground.

'I'm going back,' said Tina. 'I bet she never went beyond that first crossing.' 'I'll go on up to the gate,' said Keith. 'She might be waiting up there.'

Off they cantered. Penny and I stayed where we were and shouted. Our voices echoed back as if to mock us. Tina returned. 'No sign of her,' she said. So we sat in the silent fog and waited for Keith... and he didn't come back either.

Eventually the three of us set off towards the gate, wondering what he might have found... or whether he'd met up with misfortune, too, and in turn hadn't been able to stop Kestrel. We intended to trot. We couldn't see a thing in the fog and any moment Kestrel might be coming back towards us. But Mio wasn't going to be left out of all this dashing about: this was one of the times when I was still unable to hold him.

Off up the track he roared. Nutty and Kelly in pursuit, and sure enough suddenly, out of the fog, came Kestrel. We reined like troopers: we were getting pretty good at it: we certainly got enough practice. 'She isn't up at the gate,' reported Keith. 'I've been looking round for tracks, but there's just no sign of her anywhere.'

We started back for the stables. Obviously there'd have to be a search party and the sooner it got started the better. Lynn Hutchings, for instance, knew every inch of the moors, and as an expert rider would cover it faster than any of us. We'd have to call the police, too. Probably they'd bring in tracker dogs. Where was the nearest point to the road, to get a stretcher? We looked at the various sidetracks as we rode back the way we'd come, but decided against trying any of them. There were so many. We could so easily miss her in the fog. Better to get straight back and get an organised search started.

Which was how we came to meet up with her. Sitting patiently on Barbary, in the fog, at the crossing where we'd first expected to see her. She'd waited for us, she said – Barbary had been perfectly under control – then she'd heard us thundering up the track, so she'd taken him up a side-path so he wouldn't be set off again by our coming. And there she'd sat like a Sioux scout while the four of us shot past... hidden from us by a swirl of mist, no doubt: certainly we hadn't seen her. She'd gone on then, intending to take a short cut and catch us up, which must have been how Tina missed her... but the fog had thickened so she had turned back, reckoning that we would, too, when we couldn't find her.

We rode back silently for a while, limp with relief, then I began to laugh. 'What's so funny?' asked Tina. 'Only that Mrs Hutchings is supposed to be looking after *us*,' I said. 'You'd think we were teaching *her*!'

# Four

NOTHING EVER HAPPENS IN our village without somebody being around to see it. Fred Ferry, for instance, had been in the forest that day in the mist. Don't ask me why, except that he always seems to be up there, just as Father Adams appears to live perpetually in ambush over our garden wall.

'He says,' said Father Adams, coming in to tell us what Fred had been broadcasting up in the Rose and Crown... 'he says thee wust careerin' about up there like a buzz-fly under a meat-cover 'n he wondered whatever was goin' on. 'N then he seed thic bloke come tearin' out of the fog and the rest of thee stop dead with thee in front, and he realised what tothers was doin' was tryin' to stiffen thee nerve.'

It was no use trying to put him right. There is an amazing echo in the valley. Often I've stood in the cottage garden and heard the sound of horses galloping up on one of the forest tracks. So clearly that I could tell how many there were, where they started cantering and when they stopped again, and hear the riders' voices calling to each other. In the same way, so many people had heard our carryings-on during the time of the trials with Barbary... the sounds of frenzied galloping, the yells to 'Look out!' and 'For heaven's sake *hold* him!'... they had no difficulty in believing Fred Ferry's version and the story went round like wildfire.

'You've got yourselves insured for this trip, have you?' asked one of our neighbours – looking at me, I noticed, not at Charles – while Miss Wellington, when it got to her ears, came scurrying down immediately; the first time we'd seen her in weeks.

She was so worried, she said. If only she'd spared more time for us she might have persuaded us not to be so rash as to think of going. As we knew, though, she'd had other things on her mind... though thank goodness that was all settled now.

We were glad to hear it. When Miss Wellington gets intense about something the oddest situations are likely to ensue. One result of the arrival of the Bannetts, for instance, had been that when the Rector went to call on her one day he couldn't find anywhere to put his hat. All eight pegs of Miss Wellington's hallstand, usually chastely garnished with her gardening hat, her shopping hat and her sou-wester, were festooned with men's headgear. Trilbies, cloth caps, a dented bowler... the Rector was quite startled, wondering what had happened until out bustled Miss Wellington, whipping off the hats like a pile of pancakes, exhorting him to please hang his up *anywhere*, these were only there to scare off strangers.

Including, obviously, the Bannetts. It seemed that Miss Wellington had a cousin in town who always kept a man's hat on her hallstand to ward off intruders and Miss Wellington, inspired by this and carrying it as usual to excess, had decided that eight hats would be even better. She'd bought them at a jumble sale and the effect was quite spectacular. Understandable when she explained it, as she did to the Rector, but pretty rivetting when spotted by the milkman, or by people peering in as they passed.

Some interesting theories had gone round about those hats, particularly since Miss Wellington, to add authenticity to their being there, had taken to opening her back door and shouting 'Frank' into the garden at odd intervals... followed, according to some observers, by her creeping along the hedge between her cottage and the Bannetts' at dusk with one of the hats bobbing above it on a stick. Fred Ferry, of course, insisted he'd seen a real bloke. 'Different 'un every night,' he elaborated, capitalising on the fact of the several hats, and though nobody believed him for a moment it was just as well, rumour adding to itself as it does, that Miss Wellington had come to the end of that particular little fantasy. Or at least, we hoped she had.

What had led her to the discovery that the Bannetts were, as she put it, 'like us,' was her worrying, after several weeks had passed, because she hadn't conformed to village etiquette and called on them. Few people had. For one thing both of them worked and were away all day; for another, people don't do this calling business quite so much these days; for a third they were undoubtedly a *bit* odd... So far as we were concerned this would have been a reason *for* calling, having the reputation of being odd ourselves, except that we'd been so busy getting ready to go to Canada... Anyway having worried herself into her usual state of expecting to be punished by the Almighty at any moment if she didn't forthwith do whatever it was she had left undone. Miss Wellington had tapped timidly on the Bannetts' door one evening bearing a bottle of her elderflower wine. Liz had asked her in, and when she saw six tortoises basking in a semi-circle in the Bannetts' fireplace, her doubts, she told us earnestly, had been stilled immediately.

Most people's doubts would more likely have increased, particularly since each of the tortoises was tucked up separately in a bedroom slipper. Not Miss Wellington's however. 'That dear boy has loved tortoises since he was a child,' she informed us rapturously. 'There was one at his infant school, in the sandpit, that wasn't being cared for properly, and he insisted, even then, on taking it home and looking after it himself. And that dear girl puts them into slippers to keep them off the flagstone floor. They bring them in from their pen at night because a couple of them have colds... and those two dear things light a fire every evening to keep the tortoises warm.'

Also, to keep the record straight, because they were thrilled with their open fireplace and liked to see a log fire burning in it. It was a long time yet to winter and the tortoises provided a good excuse – though there was no doubt either that they liked the heat. We saw them ourselves in due course. Six slippers fanned out in front of the fire, a small tortoise already asleep in two of them – and four big ones doggedly trying to clamber over each other on to the hearthstone, heads outstretched to what must have seemed to them like the warmth of the Caribbean, while Liz prepared hot milk for the pair that had the colds.

Add to that the fact that the Bannetts not only liked her elderflower wine but had embarked on making it themselves... their inglenook, where it wasn't occupied by tortoises, was now packed with glugging gallon jars plus a couple of carboys for good measure... and Miss Wellington was well away. Tim with that beard, she told us, looked exactly like the photograph of her father as a young man that hung over the tallboy in her bedroom... and had I noticed that the long red string of Florentine beads that Liz wore was just like the one she had herself, only hers was blue? I had. As I'd noticed that there wasn't much difference in the vaguely flowering dresses the pair of them wore, either, except that Miss Wellington's were the real vintage twenties and Liz's were mod-shop copies. Pass for mother and daughter they would... or rather for niece and slightly dotty great-aunt. Miss Wellington's ship had really come home. She had a pair of young fledglings to fuss over.

So had we. Four of them to be exact. Still happily occupying our garage with their parents and, with a fortnight to go to our departure date, showing no sign whatever of vacating it. The garage door still leant against the plum-tree with Father Adams and his cronies passing comment on it – though to be honest, by this time we were beset by so many other pitfalls that a garage without a door was the least among our worries.

Shebalu had started the ball rolling, four weeks before we were due to go, by being sick and refusing to eat. This was a phenomenon in itself. At two years old she'd never been known to miss a meal in her life and usually had to be shut in the hall while Seeley, who was a slow eater, finished, or she'd have polished off his as well. After a day of watching her languish round the place like Camille... sitting in the middle of the floor looking fragile; turning her head wanly when we offered her food; answering us, when we spoke to her, in a faint little voice that indicated she was going any moment now but she forgave us for being Unkind to her... we called the Vet. We couldn't take a chance, we told him. If she was incubating anything we must know at once. Not only would we not go away if she were ill but, even if she meanwhile fully recovered, she certainly couldn't go to Low Knap because of the danger to other cats.

Not to worry, he said after he'd examined her. His bet, bearing in mind the hot weather, was that she'd either been catching flies and eating them, or food on which a fly had pitched. He'd give her an injection by way of precaution, but he was sure it was just a passing stomach upset. If it was catching, Seeley would give us an indication fast enough, he added encouragingly. He'd go down with it too, probably within a week.

That then, took care of the fourth week from departure date. Watching over Shebalu, feeling like jumping for joy when she at last sniffed faintly at my finger dipped in salmon paste... sniffed it again and then began to lick with fervour... and then concentrating our vigil on Seeley. It still *could* have been an infection which Shebalu had taken only lightly. Any moment now Seeley, too, could go off his food.

He didn't. No more, anyway, than was occasioned by his indignation when he found me hanging around watching him every time he attempted to eat. Why was I doing That? he kept on wailing at me aggrievedly. Didn't I know it put him Off? Couldn't he even enjoy his minced pig's heart in Private?

By which time we'd arrived at three weeks prior to departure date and Charles's Aunt Ethel announced that she was dying. This in itself was not unusual. Any time for the past 20 years any of the family had gone on holiday, she always decided she was dying. Not usually on the telephone at 8.30 in the morning, though, sounding as though she was fading fast and asking weakly for Charles.

Panic-stricken I fetched him, hovering anxiously while he spoke to her. 'Put your teeth in, Aunt,' he said almost at once. (So that was the reason for the feeble old-lady voice.) 'No, you're *not* talking to an angel. Put your hearing aid in. No you haven't, otherwise I'd hear it oscillating. Put it in now. IMMEDIATELY.'

All was well, as was confirmed when, more or less normal communication having been achieved, Charles said he'd ring her doctor and she quavered that it was too late now for that. The slightest thing really wrong with her and it was the doctor who rang us. Aunt Edith having summoned him personally, not risking any delay by dealing through intermediaries. Charles checked with the doctor nevertheless – who said that she was likely to reach a hundred but he, Dr Cartwright, wasn't: not with Aunt Edith ringing him at six in the morning twice already that week to ask should she have All Bran for breakfast. And on we went to week two from departure date, when things really began to happen.

We'd been trying for months to arrange for the hire, in Canada, of a single-unit camper – the sort which carries its own water supply and refrigerator and has a made-up bed over the driving cabin. So far every firm we'd contacted was either fully booked for the season or its campers were king-size, luxury-type, and correspondingly expensive. Now, suddenly, up came CP Air with the offer of a small Mazda four-berth camper, based in Edmonton to which our flights were booked, and – it seemed like a miracle at this point of the summer – available from mid-July through to September.

The manager of CP Air's London office rang up and we clinched the deal on the spot – which achievement Charles, relieved to know that he wasn't after all going to have to sleep out on the prairie wrapped in a blanket, celebrated by going out and putting in his runner-bean sticks. Ten-and 12-foot-high hazel branches which reared skywards like teepee poles and when Ern Biggs enquired why he hadn't trimmed them off at the normal six feet – 'To encourage the beans,' Charles lightheartedly informed him. 'It'll give them something to aim for.' Ern looked at the youthful bean plants, up at the heights to which they were supposed to aspire, back again at Charles with his mouth open and headed speedily down the lane to Father Adams.

'They'll have to pick the ruddy things with a ladder', his disbelieving voice came floating up to us while Charles, already mentally at the wheel of our camper, bean-poled blissfully on.

So blissful was he that when, next day, there was a telephone call from Canada House passing on an invitation for us to be guests of the City of Edmonton for their Klondike Days festivities... and please could we let them have our measurements so that our costumes could be ready for us on arrival... Charles voted immediate acceptance of that as well.

We could hardly have turned it down seeing that the Canadian Government was sponsoring our trip but it gave me an uneasy moment or two when I considered the implications. Victorian costumes, they'd said. Charles for five whole *days* in a Victorian topper and tailcoat when he practically had to be straitjacketted to get him into tails for a three-hour wedding? Probably with a frill-fronted shirt and string tie as well, and carrying a gold-topped cane into the bargain?

Leaving, like Scarlett O'Hara, the possibilities of that situation to take care of themselves, I concurred in accepting the invitation and we swept on to one week from departure date – when Aunt Edith rang us four times in one evening with the information that she was definitely weakening and if she didn't see us again she hoped we'd enjoy ourselves; with a last minute flash of inspiration, as the swallows still showed no sign of moving out, we re-hung the garage door but removed the glass from a window high in the apex, so they could use that way in and out instead. Shebalu jumped out of our bedroom window, which I'd forgotten to close, at five o'clock one morning (that was all right too, though; she must have landed on the lawn and when I panicked downstairs to look for the body she appeared unconcernedly through the back gate, nattering happily about what a Fine Day it was and why weren't the rest of us up yet); and Charles, small wonder after all we'd been through, developed a tooth infection.

We made it though. On the allotted day, against all odds, we finally flew out to Edmonton: Charles with a supply of penicillin tablets which he had to take every four hours; me a bag of nerves in case his infection got worse in mid-Atlantic. And suddenly we could see Hudson Bay below us, and there we were. Coming down over the North-West Territories... the Athabasca River and the barren lands north of Edmonton, covered with muskeg and dotted, as far as the eye could see, with hundreds of little lakes that looked, from the air, like puddles... And finally Edmonton itself, its tall buildings golden in the late afternoon sunlight, and beyond it the Canadian prairie, rolling away to the south.

# Five

WE COULD HARDLY BELIEVE it. We remembered Edmonton from two years previously as an outstandingly modern city. The Oil Capital of Canada, with more than seven thousand producing oil wells within a hundred-mile radius. A city of wide streets, beautiful buildings, a magnificent University complex perched high above the North Saskatchewan River and an energetically youthful population – 72 per cent of them under forty years of age, according to statistics – whose brisk-looking brief-cased businessmen travelled by air-bus to Calgary or Vancouver as matter-of-factly as Brighton residents catch a train to London.

Now, driving into it in the airport limousine, we seemed to have gone eighty years back in time. A stagecoach passed us, creaking on its springs, a guard with a shotgun sitting beside the driver. Women swept along the pavements in bustles and flower-piled hats as though they had never in their lives worn anything else. The streets themselves looked odd... suddenly we realised what it was. The buildings had false painted fronts. Wooden-fronted saloons, a barber's shop with red-and-white striped pole, an old-time jail... the Hertz rent-a-car offices disguised as stables, offering mules for hire. Tied up at the Bank of Montreal's entrance, where a sign said 'Deposit Your Gold Here,' there actually was a mule, complete with prospector's kit of pick, shovel, gold-panning sieve and bedroll.

Another mule was tethered outside the Château Lacombe hotel where we were to stay – where the traffic was held up, to let the bus turn into the courtyard, by a frock-tailed Victorian policeman with a truncheon at his belt and where, standing in the hotel lobby while Charles registered us in, I felt like the principal character in one of those Bateman cartoons. Me in scarlet trouser suit and big sling air-bag and every other person in the lobby straight out of frontier history.

Even the group of businessmen emerging from one of the hotel conference rooms were in the appropriate gear. Magenta, dove-grey and powder-blue tailcoats, peg-top trousers and elastic-sided boots. Not one of them looked in the least self-conscious, either, as one would expect men to be in such clothes – because, it seems, they do this every year and would look more incongruous if they didn't.

It is Edmonton's way of remembering the famous Gold Rush of 1898, when the city, then little more than a Hudson's Bay fur trading post halfway to the frozen north, became important overnight as one of the bases for miners heading for the Klondike. As a realistic way of commemorating history – not by speeches and exhibitions but by a halcyon, rip-roaring fortnight in July when Edmonton goes into costume en masse... when roulette wheels turn in saloons again, waiters in striped aprons scuttle around carrying clutches of beer mugs, go into a bank and you'll be served, without his turning a hair, by a cashier wearing straw boater, butcher-striped waistcoat and sleeve-garters – there can be few experiences to equal it.

Our own costumes were waiting for us in our room and I, one of my lifelong dreams being to have lived in the gay Nineties, was into mine like a shot. So was Charles, without a word of protest... in fact he appeared to be rather pleased with himself. We surveyed each other. He in an olive-green tailcoat, green-striped trousers, kingfisher-blue brocade waistcoat, buff top-hat and gold-topped cane, I in a pink slipper-satin Mae West dress with a huge cartwheel hat trimmed with ostrich feathers. 'Whoever would have thought a trip to see Canadian Wildlife would start like this,' said Charles. 'What on earth would the village think if they could see us now?'

What indeed. Particularly in the days that followed, when Charles, entering thoroughly into his Victorian dandy role, sang a microphone duet at a public luncheon with Klondike Kate, and he and I, together with David Hunn, the Sports Correspondent of *The Observer*, danced Knees Up Mother Brown, by request of the audience, on the stage of the Silver Slipper Saloon. As Britishers – the only ones in the party of writers and photographers – apparently we added authenticity to the occasion. I lost my shoes, Charles practically dislocated himself, but we did the British pioneers of the 1890s proud!

The whole thing was like a dream. One morning we had breakfast with the Mounties. Not the khaki-shirted RCMP of modern times with their peaked caps and streamlined police cars, but men in the scarlet tunics, blue riding breeches and wide-brimmed hats that represented law on the prairies in the old days. It reminded me irrepressibly of a scene from *Rose Marie* – with due apologies to the Mounties themselves, who wince at the name of Nelson Eddy!

Sitting at a huge round table, eating bacon and eggs and muffins and honey, we talked of horses and riding and of being out on the trail. Even so, when I kicked what I thought was some dropped cutlery and bent to pick it up, and realised that in fact it was the jingling of my neighbour's spurs... sturdy silver spurs with chains on them, fastened to the traditional black RCMP riding boots ... it brought home to me with a surge of joy that I was back in my beloved West. Even in the cities the outdoors is not very distant.

Certainly not in Edmonton, where from the window of our hotel room we could look out, beyond the tall white buildings and wide, straight-running streets, to where the prairie waited for us. A mist of burnt-yellow and blue in the distance, stretching on as far as the eye could see. Five days to go before we set out on our own trail. Meanwhile we enjoyed our Klondike Days.

We did enjoy them, too. Normally we live quiet country lives. Sophistication is not our cup of tea. But this sophistication... the nightclubs, the receptions, the huge luncheon given by the Toronto and Dominion Bank... all of it was overlaid with a country-style flavour that was irresistible, like a gigantic Harvest Home that just went on and on. Country-style, yet tempered with old-time elegance. Wearing those costumes seemed to have an effect on people. Women moved with grace, men became much courtlier... opening doors, doffing their toppers with a flourish, bowing the ladies through. Which is how Charles, who is always courtly, made history at the Château Lacombe.

Charles always ushers ladies through turn-stiles and doorways ahead of him. The number of times I've gone through a theatre foyer or a Customs barrier with Charles, as I think, right behind me... and when the official holds out his hand and I turn to indicate my husband, who has the tickets or our joint passport, as the case may be, there he is, with about eight females between me and him, politely waving them on...

It was a foregone conclusion, therefore, that Charles in 1890s costume would be courtlier than ever. Always last out of the hotel lift, for instance, having ushered everybody out ahead of him – though normally it didn't matter in the least. Usually our party filled the whole of the lift and we all got out at the same floor.

On this occasion, however, we had an additional couple on board. In Klondike costume, of course, so nobody really noticed. And at our appointed floor our party trooped out, dispersing towards its various rooms. We had ten minutes flat in which to freshen up and meet again, ready for the next sortie, down in the hotel lobby.

The rest of the party dispersed, that is. As I stood there waiting for Charles to come out of the lift he politely gestured the remaining pair to precede him, the woman stepped forward in her aquamarine bustle... pressed the lift button with the point of her parasol and, right before my very eyes, the lift doors closed and off soared Charles.

Apparently, the next thing was that Charles explained he'd wanted to get out there, and the woman tried to halt the lift by running her finger down all the buttons from top to bottom before he or her husband could stop her. This produced the galvanising effect (the couple themselves getting out two floors up) that the lift, with Charles as its solitary occupant, went on stopping at every floor, right on up to the twenty-fourth with the revolving restaurant on the top, and then began to descend again, opening and closing at every stop.

On the way up the doors had parted to reveal a man in a maroon frock-coat standing on one of the landings, waiting for a downward lift. He didn't half look surprised, said Charles, when the doors opened on the downward descent and there was Charles, still in solitary glory, now on his way down. Even more surprised when, he having pressed the button for the lobby, the lift continued to stop and open automatically at every floor going down. Nobody was waiting to get in, of course; it was the result of the woman pressing all the buttons.

Unfortunately Charles got so engrossed in explaining this that when the lift eventually arrived back at the twelfth floor Charles didn't realise it and so didn't get out. I wasn't on the landing to signal to him, being busy, by that time, trying to find a maid with a key to our room... our ten minutes' breather was nearly up and we were due down in the lobby almost at once. And so it was that when Charles, having descended floor by floor to the lobby where a fascinated audience had gathered to watch the phenomenal progress of the lift flashes, smiled at them disarmingly and started back up again... when he eventually arrived once more at the twelfth floor and the door opened upon the landing, the rest of our party was gathered there, waiting now to go down.

Unruffled, courteous as ever, Charles stood aside to let them get in. 'Oh no you don't!' I said, grabbing him before he could do it again.

It was that afternoon, following lunch at the Old Spaghetti Factory which we made, thanks to the lift descent, by the skin of our teeth, that we met our first-ever grizzly. Not in the remoteness of the Rockies, as we'd expected, but in a Game Park fifteen miles from Edmonton. And if that sounds tame... it isn't if you do as I did, and feed a full-grown grizzly with a feeding bottle. One of the biggest grizzlies in captivity, weighing six times as much as a man.

It was the idea of the Edmonton Travel Manager, with whom we'd been talking over our plans. There were wolves in Jasper National Park, he told us – though we'd be lucky if we saw them in the summer. There were grizzlies in the mountains around Waterton... we knew that for ourselves, of course. We'd heard stories about them on our previous visit. It was one of the reasons we were going back to Waterton. But, said the Travel Manager, if we went out to the Alberta Game Farm we could talk with experts on the subject. They could tell us a lot about them. They actually had three full-grown grizzlies, and Canadian lynx and cougar, and deer and prairie buffalo.

They did, and the sight of the animals in their natural surroundings is one we shall long remember. I don't like zoos, but the Game Farm is something different, with such large enclosures that in many of them you can't see the boundaries. Some of the animals there would be extinct by now but for dedicated projects like this, striving for their protection. Particularly we were impressed by the colony of timber wolves, safe there from poisoning or shooting, wandering, reticent from people as is their inclination, in the distance among the trees, on their vast, well-wooded hillside. I shall always remember being studied, too, by the intelligent eyes of a huge grizzly bear, his face no more than a foot from mine.

He was one of a trio of orphaned cubs found eleven years previously in the Swan Hills country, which lies to the north-west of Edmonton. There had long been stories of a particularly large type of grizzly in this region, believed to be pure descendants of the long-extinct Plains Grizzly. The largest grizzly ever recorded in Canada had come from the Swan Hills. Shot by a mountain guide thirty years before, it reared, when mounted as it would stand when facing up to a man, to more than ten feet high.

Now however, with oil being discovered there in increasing quantities and the oil companies moving in to set up camps and bulldoze roads, the Swan Hill grizzlies were being exterminated. Shot as they puzzedly tried to follow their old trails, or as they wandered in, as bears have a penchant for doing, to feed at the campsite garbage dumps. The advent of the three cubs, found by an Indian trapper who walked sixty miles to the nearest settlement to phone the Director, was a great day for the Alberta Game Farm.

When the cubs arrived, Big Dan, the male of the trio, weighed seven pounds and his sisters, Lady Edith and Swanie, weighed five and four pounds respectively. Brought up by bottle, eleven years later Big Dan weighed nearly a thousand pounds (the weight of six 11-stone men) and his sisters were pretty big too. They were fed on meat, eggs, lettuce, bread, pastries and carrots... but still they had their daily milk bottles.

To ensure they got their individual requirements of vitamins, explained the naturalist who took us round, they'd had these in their bottles as cubs and if now they just had a communal tub of milk in their pen, the male would drink the lot and get all the vitamins. So they still had their daily bottles. Being hand-fed helped to keep them tame – and a short while before this had solved a perilous situation.

It seemed that someone had left the door of their enclosure open and the bears, by nature inquisitive, had discovered this and promptly walked out. When spotted they were padding, past the other enclosures, looking in at the animals, and the Game Park staff held its breath. Tame they ostensibly were, but grizzlies are notoriously unpredictable. If they once got the killing lust nothing would stop them. They could kill an animal – or a man – with one blow.

So the naturalists fetched their rifles and took up strategic positions as the bears shambled one behind the other along the paths. Was this to be the end of all the years of work – having to shoot their charges deliberately?

In some places, with panic and less understanding, it might have been. Here, however, the watchers waited patiently and a little later, as it got near feeding time, the grizzlies turned, padded massively back past the pens of nervous deer... straight into their own enclosure, where they sat up on their haunches, in a row behind the chain-mesh fencing, and happily awaited their feeding bottles.

It was feeding time now. Would I like to give Big Dan his milk? enquired the naturalist. And now it was my turn for a surprise. The bottle, when it arrived, was about three feet long and held three-and-a-half gallons. I had to balance it, to feed him, on my shoulder.

The attendants sometimes feed the grizzlies actually inside the enclosure and no scene is more photographed by visitors... the huge bears sitting up, paws around the bottles, while the attendants tilt them helpfully as they empty. I, for safety's sake, fed Big Dan through the mesh. Even so, looking at his huge black claws holding the mesh at the side of my hands, his enormous head and his deep-set eyes...

eyes that gazed thoughtfully into mine from a scant 12-inch distance as he noisily sucked at his bottle... never, I thought, had I expected to get this close to a grizzly. Was it a good omen for our trip?

It must have been. When, two days later, we set out on our own trail to the Rockies, little did we guess the adventures that awaited us. Meantime we watched enthralled as the Game Farm grizzlies, having finished their milk, embarked on the business of actual feeding, padding across to where three huge piles of food awaited them – a mountain of greenstuff, another of smashed eggs, and what looked like stale doughnuts from every baker's in Edmonton. Swanie went for the lettuce. Lady Edith started on the eggs, cramming them into her mouth with both paws. My boy Big Dan? Monarch of all he surveyed, he made straight for the doughnuts.

# Six

THAT WAS ON SATURDAY. We'd changed into ordinary clothes to visit the grizzlies. We'd done a good many things the past few days in stovepipe trousers and hobble skirt but they weren't very suitable for running in. We were back in costume that evening, though, for dinner and dancing in a replica of a nineties banqueting saloon. We were in costume by six o'clock next morning, too, for the crowning event of Klondike Days... the famous Bonanza Breakfast, held on the Edmonton racecourse.

It seemed an unearthly hour to us, but outdoor social breakfasts are an old Canadian custom and as our party arrived at the racecourse entrance dead on 7.30, there were the Edmontonians in their hundreds, converging in trailing skirts and cartwheel hats, toppers and frilled shirt-fronts, to eat sausages, bacon and pancakes in the grandstand and stroll up and down in leisurely promenade watching the racehorses being exercised. The band, the gorgeous costumes, the long-legged horses flashing past on the emerald turf... it was *My Fair Lady* come to life. It was difficult for a moment to realise that this was Western Canada.

Not so that afternoon, when we watched the raft races on the North Saskatchewan River. They might look funny and they were intended to be... the rafts swirling along on the current with chicken coops on top, smoke coming out of tin-can chimneys, sails flapping from broomsticks lashed to barrels labelled Dynamite... but even they were an echo of the early days when men unable to afford any other kind of transport built rafts, put provisions, furniture and often their families and livestock on board, and poled their way to a new land-stake up the great rivers of the West.

The melodrama we saw that evening at the theatre... that, too, was a projection of the past, with the audience cheering the heroine, enthusiastically stamping at the hero, and throwing over-ripe fruit at the villain, who promptly hurled it back. It could so easily have been a real frontier show, and we prospectors about to leave for the Klondike.

What we were about to leave for, however, were those grizzlies. Next day, relinquishing our costumes with considerable nostalgia... it had felt all this time as though we really were living in the past and we were reluctant to leave it for the present... we headed for the Kentwood Ford offices on the outskirts of Edmonton to pick up our camper.

Our spirits soared as soon as we saw it – as compact as a ship's galley with sink, cooker and refrigerator on one side, a furnace on the other for cold nights in the mountains, bench seats and a movable table in the body of the camper, a big double bed up in front over the driving cab (one stood on a seat to get into it) and more cupboards than we could possibly use. Towels, crockery, cutlery, pillows, sleeping bags and sheets... everything was there; all new and sealed in polythene bags, Canadians being particular. One entered the camper up folding iron steps at the rear, like an old-fashioned gypsy caravan, and there was a hatchway at the front end for communication through to the driving cabin. Looking at our home for the next six weeks, visualising it out on the prairie, by the rivers, in the great Canadian forests, we knew that this, after all, was what we'd come for. City life may be fine for a while but, at any rate for us, there is nothing like the great outdoors. With a vehicle like this... self-contained, independent... like a couple of Columbuses we could go anywhere.

The first place these Columbuses had to go, however, was back to the Château Lacombe to collect our luggage and, seeing that it meant driving through crowded down-town Edmonton at lunch-time on the (to us) wrong side of the road, in a vehicle the size of a small removal van, with left-hand drive, Charles, I thought, did superbly.

Modestly he said it was easy. Anyone could handle a camper like this. True, at one stage we went three times round the block on Jasper Avenue... in that traffic build-up anyone might do it twice but the policeman on point duty didn't half look surprised when, having waved us accommodatingly round on two occasions, back we came a few minutes later still signalling right. True, having eventually left Edmonton behind us... travelling westwards, as we thought, on the Yellowhead Highway towards Jasper... we discovered we were in fact heading directly northwards, straight for the Arctic Circle... but those were my faults. I was doing the navigating. And eventually, having gone back once again to Edmonton (there are no interconnecting roads round cities in the Canadian West and North; one exits from them on highways built on the old fur-traders' trails... North, South, East or West and never do any of them meet), there we were, with a week's supply of food aboard, driving determinedly towards the Rockies.

We camped that first night in a forest clearing – designated as a Highways campsite but as unlike the English idea of a camping ground as one could possibly imagine. No euphemistic 'toilet block'; merely two log-built chemical closets in the trees beyond the clearing with bear warnings tacked up on the doors. No water tap: just a pump which spouted well-water in a corner. No site-shop selling the milk and bread so essential to English campers, and in consequence no huddling together of caravans for the night, either.

Only one other vehicle pulled in later into the furthest corner of the clearing, the occupants emerging to light a campfire and cook steaks and brew coffee on it, and while to a degree we regretted even that... nobody around for miles is our idea of camping... I must admit to a certain relief in the thought that if a bear did happen along while I was in that little log hut among the trees (with my aptitude for encounters, if there was one within a mile he certainly would)... there were other people around if I had to shout for rescue.

Not that Charles wouldn't have tackled it on his own, and unless the bear was angry it would have been simple. Black bear, the only type likely to be round there, normally take to their heels if anyone shouts at them. Don't antagonise them. Don't ever get between a female bear and her cubs.

If you are holding food, throw it down and back away if they come towards you. These – and keeping an eye open for a handy tree – are the salient points to remember in bear country. I knew all this from our previous visit and nobody had been more full of aplomb than I in talking about bears in England. It was a different matter, though, our first night out from civilisation. Out there in that lonely log privy, shining a tremulous torch on the bear warning and listening to odd crackling noises outside in the forest, I wasn't half glad that Charles stood on guard outside the door and that over in the clearing, their campfire reflecting comfortingly through the privy latch-hole, was a Canadian family no doubt used to dealing with bears.

Within a few days we were back to being used to them ourselves. By this time we were ensconced in the Wapiti campground in Jasper National Park and if that scarcely sounds like adventurous camping I should point out that the Park is 4,200 square miles in area, a large part of this is wilderness country where only naturalists and the more intrepid go, and that 'park' merely means that it is patrolled by rangers and that within its boundaries all animal, bird and plant life is protected. Much of it is dense natural forest and as a safeguard against starting fires, all vehicles must be parked at night in one of the official campgrounds.

We had hoped that, being on a semi-official trip, we might be permitted to camp out of laager. It wasn't allowed, said the warden If one did it everybody would want to and they'd have dozens of forest fires to deal with every morning. So we were allotted a site from the chart in the warden's office – a small clearing fringed with saskatoon bushes, wild raspberries and cottonwood trees, on the edge of the Athabasca River. The clearing contained the rough-hewn log table and fireplace which are features of most Canadian campsites... the table for the camper's convenience, the fireplace – a large iron box with a grille standing a few inches off the ground – compulsory for the lighting of fires so as to keep them under control.

We lit our fire, we cooked our supper, we ate it at our log table by the Athabasca River. Owls hooted in the forest. In from of us the river rushed and gurgled. Through the trees we could see the glow of other campfires. Barring the refinements of the table and fireplace, we reflected, the early explorers might have camped in such a place as this, listening to the roaring of the river and wondering what lay out there in the darkness.

How right we were we learned next morning when a passing ranger, stopping for a chat while we were cooking breakfast, asked if we knew we were on La Grande Traverse. That's it, right there in front of you,' he said, indicating the narrow track that ran along the river bank a few feet from our camper door. We stared, scarcely able to believe it. The most famous of all the old Hudson Bay Company's trade routes. 'Shades of the *Boy's Own Paper*', said Charles. To think we're actually on it!'

I was raised on *The Magnet* myself, but I knew just how he was feeling. This way, in their time, had come explorers, fur-traders, prospectors... on foot or with plodding pack-horse train along this very path. Up-river, through the Athabasca Pass in the mountains, by canoe down the Columbia River to the coast. A journey that took weeks, sometimes months, to accomplish. Some of those travellers must have camped on this very spot.

That, and the fact that the warden told us we were within twenty miles of wolf country... he'd arrange for us to go up there with a naturalist if we liked... sold Wapiti to us. We camped there for a week. We saw several bears and we heard the wolves. The reason we didn't see them was that they are afraid of human beings.

It is a fact. Those hair-raising adventure stories in which wolves attack the hero... being held off by his waving a firebrand at them or chasing a racing sleigh from which, with his last remaining shot, he valiantly downs the leader... have no foundation whatever. Wolves, like dogs, are basically friendly towards humans... or would be, given the chance.

Years ago they say, back in the days before the settlers came, it was a common occurrence to meet up with a wolf. A traveller might come across one lying asleep in the sun or under a bush... it was the wolf which leapt to its feet in alarm and then, seeing the intruder was a man, would raise its tail and pad placidly away. The Indians regarded the wolves as their friends. There were even individuals who claimed to understand their language and to be able to communicate with them, the wolves warning them of approaching danger.

Fantastic though it may sound there is now confirmation of this. Parley Mowat in his book *Never Cry Wolf*, for instance, records several instances of an Eskimo being able to interpret what wolves were saying. In one case a dog wolf told his mate that the hunting was bad and he wouldn't be returning till the middle of the day (in fact, says Parley Mowat, the wolf came back at 12.17). On another occasion the Eskimo said a distant wolf was telling one close at hand that travellers coming from the north-west were passing through his territory. In due course, the Eskimo having gone out to meet them on the strength of the wolf's message, the travellers came into camp. The wolf who had received the message, and who normally went hunting to the north-west, had meanwhile gone in the opposite direction, obviously to avoid them.

Of the wolf's compatibility with man we'd seen evidence on our previous visit. Driving down into Montana, on our way to Glacier National Park, we'd stopped off in a hamlet called St. Mary's to visit a Blackfoot Indian wood-carver. Every one of his carvings was a masterpiece. A group of rearing horses, a leaping cougar, running deer... What really took my eye, however, was a series of long relief panels hanging round the walls. Scenes from old Blackfoot life, he told us. Tales he'd been told as a boy by his grandmother.

One of them raised my eyebrows a bit. Opinion now is that the Indians were wrongly treated – that it was the white men who were the villains of the piece in frontier days – and in principle this is right. In the panel showing Blackfoot warriors behind a lookout rock on a hillside however, watching a stagecoach rolling in a cloud of dust across the plain below... one of the Indians pointing down at it, another excitedly beckoning others, all of them stripped to breech clouts and armed to their Indian teeth... it hardly looked as if they planned to go down bearing a banner with 'Welcome' on it: they looked more like practised swatters watching the progress of a fly. I would like to have asked how the episode ended, but I thought it might be indiscreet. We are talking about wolves, anyway. There was this other panel on the wall...

It depicted Blackfoot hunters returning from the chase – small boys coming out to escort them, two of the hunters carrying a deer on a pole, and what appeared to be a dog trotting proudly alongside. 'A husky?' I asked, noticing that the dog was thick-set and had a ruff. 'A wolf,' said the carver matter-of-factly.

I knew they'd crossed dogs with wolves, of course. It was an old Indian and Eskimo custom to tether an in-season bitch away from the camp at night in the hope that a dog-wolf would come and mate with her. It was thought to infuse strength and stamina into her pups; wolf crosses made some of the best sledge dogs. But pure wolf? Oh yes, said the Blackfoot carver. The hunters used to bring the cubs home to the women, who raised them along with the children. They grew up perfectly tame and were very much prized as hunting dogs. Indians had never been afraid of wolves. It was the white men who were scared.

# Seven

SETTLERS FROM EASTERN EUROPE started it. Coming from closely populated countries where the wolves, unable to find wild prey, habitually raided village sheepfolds in winter... where glimpses of their dark shapes slipping through the woods and folklore about their carrying off children had terrified the peasants for ages... the immigrants took their fears and superstitions to North America with them. When they saw a wolf their policy was to kill it. English settlers, with no experience of wolves themselves, accepted the beliefs of their European neighbours. There were good inducements for killing wolves in any case. The Government paid a bounty on them, and prime wolfskins were valuable.

They were slaughtered by shooting, by trapping, by poison... In the old days, they say, when an Indian killed a buffalo or deer for food, he would often be surrounded by a circle of friendly wolves, sitting at a respectful distance, waiting for him to take what he wanted of the meat so they could move in and feed on the remnants. All the bounty-hunters needed to do with wolves like those, for a start, was to put strychnine into the carcass.

One observer, writing in the 1860s, tells of seeing ten wolves waiting in this way while their meat was poisoned for them. It was the running season, he said – the time for courting and choosing mates – and the group contained several young bitches, each with a following of dog wolves who frolicked and fawned around her. They waited as confidently as dogs, used to doing this from cubhood. Then the poisoner moved away and they frolicked in to their deaths.

Even while wolf-phobia was at its height, however, there were some people who tried to spread the truth. The man travelling through Western Nebraska, for instance, who recorded that while sleeping out in the open one night he'd been awakened by something being drawn across his chest. Opening his eyes, he found a wolf sitting by him, pawing at him as a dog might do to attract its owner's attention. He was under no illusion that the wolf was trying to be friendly. His interpretation was that it was investigating to see if he was dead or not – preparatory, if he was, to a midnight feast. The point was that the wolf made no attempt to attack him. It made off as soon as he sat up.

Over the years it has gradually been proved that a wolf will never attack a human unless cornered, and then only in a desperate attempt to escape. There has never been a single authenticated instance of anyone being killed by a wolf in North America. Probably, if the truth were known, it never happened in Europe either.

As for people's fears about wolves attacking children – a Canadian scientist who studies captive wolves has put the record straight about that. One day an inquisitive toddler in his family got, by accident, into an enclosure with wolves who'd never seen a human child before. When the alarmed adults rushed to the rescue (after all, even a dog will bite if it gets its tail pulled) the youngster was rolling about inside the wire with a big she-wolf and her cubs – and she was wagging her tail and licking him as if he was one of the pups.

The idea of wolves as savage predators, killing other animals for the love of killing, has similarly been proved to be wrong. Wolves kill only when they are hungry, say modern observers – and then, chasing a herd of deer or caribou, it is the old and lame, and the frailest of the youngsters, who fall behind and are brought down. These would die lingeringly in the winter anyway, and the culling of them is nature's way of ensuring a healthy herd. Moreover the other animals know when the wolves are really hunting and only then will they start to run. At other times a pack may travel through a valley in which caribou are grazing, and the deer will do no more than raise their heads and watch them idly as they pass.

We heard so much about them from the naturalists at Jasper... facts such as that wolves mate for life, that they are the most devoted of parents and that in any pack there will be only one breeding pair... the dominant male and female, thus ensuring the strongest offspring, the rest of the pack acting as guardians and bringers-home of food... that we'd willingly have travelled anywhere in the hope of actually seeing them.

Unfortunately, said the warden, there was little chance of that. Now they are protected the wolves are increasing in Jasper, but there are still only about six or seven packs in the Park. Living in the remotest areas, they are sometimes seen by travellers in winter. Never in the summer, though. Experience has taught them to keep away from men. The best he could offer was a night-trip into their territory in the hope of hearing them call.

One of the naturalists would take along a tape-recording of another pack howling. He'd amplify it into the night and if we were lucky, we'd hear a reply.

We went on the Saturday and it was a memorable day altogether. We spent the afternoon high in the mountains at Maligne Lake where we saw a bear-warning chewed by a porcupine (they climb the poles and eat chunks out of the board because they like the turpentine in the paint); a picnic party by the lake complete with the family cat on a tremendous length of string (the notices also warn you that dogs and cats, for safety, must be kept on leads at picnic sites and in no circumstances taken on the trail); and our first black bear of the trip.

We saw him in a clearing in which, having been told by one of the naturalists that he had seen a lynx on several occasions, we sat camouflaged in the long grass for ages, hoping to see it ourselves. Normally lynx are shy but this one, said the naturalist, wasn't bothered about people at all. Only a few days previously he'd been lecturing a group about moose, the Maligne Lake area being one of their haunts and, noticing his audience staring past him as if mesmerised, he'd turned to see the lynx crossing the path right behind him. As boldly as you like, he said; this was obviously one of his crossing points and as the humans were so preoccupied...

The lynx must have been somewhere else that day. In two hours of sitting there being bitten to pieces by mosquitoes we saw no sign of it. Eventually, in desperation, I stood up and did my imitation of a Siamese cat's fighting call. At home it always brought our two on to the scene at the double. Alas, no lynx appeared in answer to the challenge. Instead, about a dozen gophers shot out of their holes and stood on their hind legs craning at us from their look-out hillocks and, a minute or so after I'd stopped calling, a bear came into the clearing.

The gophers went down their holes like snooker balls. As for us, nobody needed to remind us to look for a handy tree. We were behind the nearest one like yo-yos on elastic – in my case with a trial foot up to see if I could reach the first branch fast if I had to. After which, precautions duly taken, we held our breath and watched the bear.

It was a big one. Probably a male, since adult females usually have their cubs with them. A black bear by species, though in this case its actual colour was brown, with a lighter, mealy muzzle. If it knew we were there, it gave no sign. Just passed through the clearing with the massive padding soundlessness that is the most striking thing about a bear's walk; like the noticeable silence of a ballet dancer's shoes on a stage when for a moment there is a pause in the music. Its head swayed from side to side, short-sightedly scanning its surroundings as it went. It made a playful bound at something – probably a movement in a gopher hole. There was nothing particularly outstanding about its passage but we, behind our tree, scarcely dared breathe for excitement. Our first bear of the trip, met up with when we were on foot. If it had spotted us we'd have been up that tree in a flash.

It didn't, but we discussed the bear all the way back to the camper, all the way down the brake-testing switchback bends that led to the Jasper-Banff road, all the time I was cooking supper by the side of Medicine Lake. (The sun was setting gloriously; might as well eat here and watch it, we decided; we'd be all set then for the wolf expedition when we got back to Wapiti.) Which was how, cooking sausages, gazing out of the window at the sunset and talking to Charles about the bear, I nearly caught the camper on fire.

A saucepan sputtered into the frying pan, the fat flared up... in a moment the cooker top was a sea of leaping flames. Charles dealt with it by slapping a saucepan lid on to the frying pan. With the air cut off, the flames died down. For a moment it had looked pretty dicey, though, with the flames shooting up round the curtains over the sink. Which was why, when the wolf expedition moved out of Wapiti campground at 11 o'clock that night, our camper was last in the convoy. It was the first time we'd driven in the dark in this vehicle and Charles said he preferred to take it easy. It wasn't our camper. I'd just almost caught it on fire. He intended to return it *intact*.

We were given the route. Left along the Jasper-Banff Highway. Right up the track towards Mount Edith Cavell. Left after about a mile, where the road forked sharply. We couldn't miss it, said the naturalist. There weren't any other turnings. And about twenty miles in, we'd come to Leach Lake. The other cars would be parked in the shadows under the trees, and he'd be down at the lakeside fixing up the equipment.

That was what he thought. The camper wasn't a fast vehicle in any case and what with going uphill, and Charles driving carefully because it wasn't ours, and looking out at snow-covered mountains in the moonlight and wondering what it was that at one point went across the road ahead of us... when we got to Leach Lake and I wound down the camper window, it was to hear a pack of wolves in full song. Closer than I had ever expected. It sounded as if they were just across the lake. Yips and yaps and a solo baritone howling which was the leader of the pack giving tongue. Then, after a pause, the others came in in chorus; melodious, yet somehow spine-chilling; muted and hauntingly mournful.

'Quick!' I whispered, grabbing the tape-recorder, sliding down out of the camper cabin and heading towards the lake on tiptoe. Charles, switching off the camper lights and pocketing the keys, slid out on his side and tiptoed after me. We were almost there, the wolves howling in glorious Valkyrie chorus, when Charles had one of his thoughts. He'd just nip back and put on the camper sidelights, he said. It was last in line on the road, and if another vehicle came along in the dark...

It was no good my saying there were enough reflectors on the camper to light it up like a fairground in another car's headlights. It was no good my asking who on earth would be this far up in the mountains at this hour. Charles, following the dictates of his conscience, went back. I went with him. I definitely believed about wolves being friendly but I preferred Charles to be around when they were. So he switched on the sidelights, which also turned on the string of lights that, by law, mark the outline of large vehicles travelling at night in Canada, and there we were, twenty miles up in the mountains, suddenly lit up like a Christmas tree.

The wolves wouldn't mind it: they'd have seen lights on campers before, said Charles – and certainly there was no diminution in their howling. So he shut the camper door and we tiptoed down to the lake and discovered why our comings and goings hadn't disturbed them. What we'd been listening to wasn't the reply from the local pack. It was the naturalist sending out *his* tape-recording.

We joined the others at the lakeside and the naturalist played it again. The effect was still as though it were real, the sound being sent out across the lake by amplifier and echoing back at us from the mountains. The yip-yip-yippmgs, the drawn-out howls, the rising and falling chorus, intermittently a pregnant pause – during which our ears, attuned now to listening, marked the wind in the pines, the water lapping at the lake-edge... and suddenly, in the midst of one of the pauses, a crash from further round the lakeside and the sound of an angrily rattling chain.

Everybody jumped yards. 'Bear,' whispered the naturalist. 'Raiding a trash can at the picnic site.' There are all kinds of rubbish bins devised to beat the bears – and always, in due course, a bear who will beat the designer. This bin was one of the swinging kind, suspended by a chain from a pole, the idea being that when the bear reaches up to claw it, the bin swings out of its grasp. This bear, presumably a tall one, had evidently swiped the lid off and was now turning it upside down. He must have succeeded. There were no more bangs or chain-rattlings. The wolf chorus rose again, faded, we listened once more. This time, faintly but unmistakeably, far in the distance, we heard what we had been waiting for. The answering call of the Jasper leader, followed in chorus by the rest of the pack. Timber wolves. They really were out there in the darkness, muzzles raised towards us from the top of some rocky crag. I could scarcely believe it. *I* was listening to *wolves*? This, surely, was the most exciting moment of my life.

Doreen Tovey

Not quite it wasn't. That came a while later, after the naturalist had suggested we go on to the Athabasca Falls. We'd be closer to them there, he said, though it would mean listening above the roar of the torrent. Right-ho, said Charles. We would bring up the rear.

The tail-lights of the last of the convoy were disappearing up the track ahead of us when we discovered we hadn't got the camper keys; they were locked inside it, dangling tantalisingly from the dashboard, where Charles had left them after switching on the lights. My fault as much as his, urging him to hurry for goodness sake or we'd miss out on the wolf-howl, but that didn't alter the fact that we were stranded 20 miles up in the mountains, with no prospect of anyone realising it for hours. They wouldn't miss us at the Falls, with the wolf-listeners scattered round in the darkness. They'd be back at Wapiti it might even be next day before anyone noticed we were missing.

We shouted, we signalled frantically with our small pocket torch. It was no use; the convoy had gone. We were locked out of our camper with a bear down by the lake and a pack of wolves somewhere off in the distance. The knowledge that bears are harmless if you are careful of them... that wolves aren't the ogres they are painted and in this case were miles away... didn't exactly desert me in our predicament. It was just that I would have felt happier if the camper door were open. 'What are we going to do?' I said. 'We can't stay here all night. Even if somebody came along, they couldn't open the door.'

'I can,' said Charles. 'I've got my Scout's knife.' I should have remembered it of course. For years he's never gone on a walk without it dangling from his belt, and the times I'd chaffed him about it. What would people think? When would he grow up? What did he expect to meet in Somerset – Bengal tigers?

Never again will I laugh at that Scout's knife. I ate my words a million times while, with me shining the tiny torch on it, Charles worked away at the window. It took him an hour, inserting the blade, tapping the catch, determined not to damage the paintwork. The torch gradually faded. There was a rustling in the bushes below us. Was it that bear coming nearer?

'Get on the camper roof,' said Charles when I asked him what we should do if it was the bear and it came out to investigate.

I surveyed the roof. Apart from the fact that it was a long way up there was a snag in that suggestion. Bears are attracted by food smells and, in my agitation at the frying-pan flare-up, I'd forgotten to wind down the roof ventilator after I'd finished cooking. I could see us up there, shouting for rescue, with a bear sitting sniffing down the ventilator beside us.

*Under* the camper, I decided, and I was ready, feet positioned for the dive (the rustling was definitely getting closer), when Charles said 'I've done it!' and the quarter-window gave, and he put his arm in and opened the door.

We were in like grasshoppers. If the rustling had been the bear, presumably Charles's starting the engine halted it. We didn't stop to close the ventilator. We turned on to the track, cooking smells coming out and all.

'Phew!' said Charles as we drove down the road. 'Phew from me, too,' I said.

# Eight

WE DIDN'T TELL MISS Wellington that one. She'd insisted we let her know how we were getting on – otherwise she'd worry, she said. So, knowing Father Adams & Co. would be all agog as well, I wrote to her once a week. Not about getting locked out of the camper with a bear in the bushes, though. By the time Father Adams had said 'twas a wonder we hadn't bin et, and Fred Ferry had forecast that we would be next time, and Ern Biggs had no doubt added that *he* knew somebody what was et by a bear. Miss Wellington would have been flat on her back on her front path, letter in senseless hand.

So I told her about hearing the wolves call and the moonlight on the fir-fringed lake, and the glacier the Indians call the Great White Ghost on the side of Mount Edith Cavell, and (since she'd worry equally if we didn't mention bears at all; we must be holding something back,

she'd insist) I told her about the extrovert one we saw
sitting in a lake the next day.

It was up at Pyramid Lake. We'd gone there for a swim
and, it being a hot Sunday afternoon with lots of people
around and the lake a very popular one, only two miles
from Jasper townsite, it was the last place we expected to
see a bear, because they don't usually frequent crowded
areas in daylight

It was the usual layout for a popular picnic spot, with
grassy clearings among the trees around the lake, most of
them occupied by family parties. What struck us, when
we found a place to park the camper, was the pile of litter,
practically knee-deep, round the nearby rubbish basket.
Probably because it was Sunday, we said. Nobody had been
round to empty it. All the same it was unlike Canadians to
be as careless with litter as that.

We changed in the camper, went in for a swim and after a
while I came out to make some tea, leaving Charles floating
blissfully on his back gazing up at Pyramid Mountain. I
was just backing down the camper steps with teapot and
cups in my hand when he came rushing up galvanised with
excitement. It was a *bear* who'd thrown that rubbish about,
he said. It was going round the lakeside turning out all the
bins and visiting the picnic parties. A man in the lake had
just told him.

Dumping the teapot – we could drink tea any time in
England – we threw on our sweaters and pants and set out
round the lake ourselves. And had that bear been busy!

In the next clearing to ours he'd swiped a big bag of buns.
They'd just put them out on the table, the picnickers told
us. Then they'd gone back to the car-boot to fetch the rest
of the stuff – and when they'd turned round, there he was!

'Jumped into the car like jackrabbits,' said the man when I asked what they'd done. 'We didn't even stop to shut down the back.' The bear had eaten the buns, looked in the empty boot... they'd taken the rest of the food into the car with them. 'Only because we were already holding it,' admitted the man, 'and we were too darned scared to drop it'.

He'd then ambled on to the next lot. He wasn't so lucky there. They hadn't got as far as setting out their meal; all they'd done was tether their tabby kitten to a nearby tree and put it down a saucer of milk. When they saw the bear they'd grabbed the kitten and leapt into their car, not even stopping to untie the other end of the tether.

The bear drank the cat's milk and proceeded on his way. In the third clearing, where the people hadn't any food at all, he just looked at them and went on through. In the fourth he ate a plate of ham and some butter. In the fifth an iced sandwich cake. He visited everybody along the lake as methodically as a ticket inspector, turning out the litter bins as well as he went. We caught up with him beyond the last of the picnic sites where a rocky outcrop marked the end of the track. Having finished his successful tour he was now cooling off in the lake, sitting upright, paws on stomach, like a patriarch at a party. Watching the bathers from a distance, neither afraid of them nor aggressive, as though he was one of the family and did it every day.

He didn't, of course. Bears like this in National Parks, who get ideas about easy food and begin to get familiar with people, are eventually doped with anaesthetic cartridges and taken out of the area by helicopter. They are released in the back country, tag-marked on the ear, so they can be recognised if they come back. They are given three chances. If a bear returns after the third fly-out it is reluctantly shot by a warden. A bear which loses its wariness of people is always a potential danger. One day, pestering for food, it may lose its temper and attack. The bear at Pyramid Lake had never been seen there before. This was something he'd just thought up We hoped he had enough sense to take off if he saw a ranger coming... and to make this his sole performance.

We left Wapiti next day. It seemed there was no chance of getting any closer to the wolves than we'd done at Leach Lake and we had a long way to go to grizzly country. Grizzlies were seen sometimes in the Jasper-Banff area but usually only in the spring. We'd have to get down to Waterton-Glacier to have a fair chance of seeing them in summer. And there we'd better watch out, one of the Jasper rangers advised us. Had we read *Night of the Grizzlies*?

We had. Waterton-Glacier is an international park, on the Alberta-Montana border. In its nearly sixty years of existence nobody had ever been fatally injured there by a bear until, in 1967, two girls were killed in one night. It had happened on the Montana side. One at Trout Lake. One nine miles away at Granite Park Chalets. In each case the girl was camping out with companions and vital rules had been broken. At Trout Lake, for instance, there was a puppy with the party and his scent was undoubtedly everywhere; particularly on the girl who was killed and her friend, who'd carried him between them when he was tired. At Granite Park the rescuers, hunting for the dragged-off victim, found a candy-bar wrapper and a packet of sweets on the trail. The girl must have taken them into her sleeping bag and a bear's nose is tuned like a tracker-dog's to sweetness: it will brave a treeful of wild bees any time for honey

There were other factors, too. It had been an exceptionally hot summer with frequent electric storms and forest fires.

This in itself could have affected the grizzlies, whose temper is always uncertain. To grizzle – to grumble,' says Chambers's dictionary – adding, surprisingly that the origin of the phrase is unknown. Anyone who has heard the muttering, menacing rumble of a grizzly knows well enough where it comes from. 'Like a bear with a sore head' is another one.

The bear at Trout Lake had been harassing and chasing people all through the summer. When tracked and shot after the tragedy it was found to be old, very thin, with worn down teeth. Raiding camps and stealing fishing catches had become easier for it than hunting and that night, apart from the lure of the campfire cooking smells, there had been the scent of dog on the girl in the sleeping bag.

At Granite Park, where there was a chalet where people could stay overnight, kitchen scraps had been dumped in a gully behind the buildings and grizzlies came regularly to feed on them. They were known to come up the trail that led past a nearby public campground. Not a campground for vehicles; the road was miles away. Hikers who stopped at this one slept in sleeping bags in the open and, despite the frequent bear traffic, no one had ever been attacked. Until the night a girl had a candy-bar in her sleeping bag and a grizzly decided it wanted it.

We'd read Jack Olsen's *Night of the Grizzlies* all right. By our campfire at Wapiti, the hair standing up on our heads. What we were doing going to that very location... but the book also gives the other side of the picture. That of the most magnificent animal on the American continent being driven, inexorably, to extinction. Hounded by bulldozers opening up its age-old territory – and, even in the parks, never with a place it can call its own. People go into grizzly country deliberately to see one

– and if they do and it chases them, they want it shot. It is only a matter of time now, say the experts, until the last wild grizzly has gone. Till the huckleberries and wild raspberries ripen on the mountain slopes and there is no great, hump-backed bear to enjoy them.

While it was still possible we wanted to see one – duly respecting its rights. So we drove southwards down through Alberta with Watenon-Glacier as our goal.

There were plenty of black bears along the road to Banff. Ambling along the wide grass verges, digging industriously in anthills (they eat the insects for the sweetness of their formic acid content), sitting up like big stuffed toys to watch us as we drove past. Occasionally one mooched with its loose-limbed walk across the road, supremely confident that people would stop for it. The bears seem to know they are safe in the parks and that the visitors enjoy their antics.

Every campground we stopped at had its fund of bear stories. At Rampart Creek they had a prize one from only the previous night. Some people had slept there in their car, with their supplies in the boat they were towing behind them. It had a heavy canvas cover which they obviously regarded as bear-proof. Not against the one who toured the campground that night it wasn't... who ripped the canvas as if it were polythene, climbed into the boat, gorged himself on biscuits, bacon and butter and then discovered to his delight that the boat-trailer had springs on it. When neighbouring campers, roused by the rhythmic creaking, looked out of their vehicles at day-break, there was the bear bouncing up and down in the boat as if he was on a trampoline, the back of the car going up and down as well – and inside it, lulled by the rocking, the people still sound asleep. 'They didn't wake up,' said the man who told us, 'till the bear went off and somebody tapped on their window. Pity they couldn't have stayed for another night. That bear in the boat was really something.'

So was the female bear they told us about at Banff, who'd taught her cubs to turn on the golf course sprinklers and take showers on hot afternoons. Every warm day without fail they'd frolicked along behind her from the ninth to the fourteenth holes, turning on the taps as they went. A grown bear doing that, as the mother was no doubt aware, would have been hauled out by helicopter in no time. But nobody could resist two playful little cubs doing it and it meant she could share the shower as well. Yes, admitted our informant, the greens *had* got a bit boggy but the golf club authorities found a way of dealing with that. They hired a boy to follow the bears at a suitably respectful distance, turning off the sprinklers when they'd finished with them.

We heard tale after tale illustrating the cleverness of bears. The one, for instance, who met up with a hiker – presumably for the first time ever – and the hiker had abandoned his pack and climbed up the nearest tree. Sitting there enjoying his haul of sandwiches and chocolate, an idea had come to that bear. Thereafter – until they took him out by helicopter – he worked a Dick Turpin act, hiding behind a bush, jumping out at hikers, hoping to scare them into throwing down their packs. They knew it was the same bear because he was always behind the same bush and eventually, anyway, people began to recognise him. He was completely harmless – if his victim didn't run away, he *did* – but they had to move him out. People complained because he would rip up their packs.

Another instance of intelligence... though whether this is actually true... was told us by a ranger discussing the subject of trash bins. Bears could master anything in his opinion, he said. He reckoned they could be taught to operate a power station. Somebody had invented a bin with a chute in it, but they'd soon learned to deal with that: they held the lid up with their heads and reached in with one of their arms... grown bears had a pretty long stretch. So, in Yellowstone Park in America, they'd thought up a trash bin to beat all trash bins. It worked like a fruit machine. You pulled a lever at the side to open it, at the same time pressing on a pedal, and for a while it did baffle the Yellowstone bears. Unfortunately it also baffled most of the campers, who took to depositing their litter around it instead of in it. Then, to beat everything, one night a naturalist saw a bear standing in front of it, his foot on the pedal, pulling the lever with his right paw and scooping out the contents with his left. 'He must have watched a human do it,' said the ranger when I asked how a bear could have worked that out. 'Honestly?' I asked a trifle doubtfully. 'Honest,' said the ranger. But as I say, we were never quite sure about that!

He was right about the copying business of course. Animals are natural mimics and at one campground they were troubled by a young bull moose which had obviously been studying the bears. That, at any rate, was the only reason they could think of for his being found continually turning out the trash bins. A moose would normally never come near a campground.

Deer, yes. At Wapiti there was a big beige buck with antlers like a Christmas tree who regularly sunned himself in a particular glade outside a large parked caravan. The people were usually away all day and, lying there like a lion on guard, it was His Glade, said his attitude; he just allowed the caravan to be there. But not a moose. They are elusive creatures but at the same time very bad-tempered. Aggravated, they will charge like a maddened bull – the danger lying not in their broad, scooped antlers but in their raking, razor-sharp hooves. They can slash another animal's throat, or open a man's back or stomach, in an instant. So, said the ranger, the moose was going to have to go. So many visitors thought it was only bears one needed to be careful of, and sooner or later somebody would try to pet him. Already he'd chased a woman into her camper because she'd run out of the bread she'd been giving him and, obviously copying some bear he'd watched, had started scrounging food off the open-air tables.

Being only a moose, they wouldn't move him out by helicopter – he'd be shot and the naturalists had grown quite fond of him... so now they were throwing logs at him whenever they saw him. Not to hit him, but to try to scare him away.

Charles and I not being dawn getter-uppers... at which time, the vigilant naturalists being asleep, several people en route to the wash-block had seen him wandering about the camp... the closest we came to him ourselves was one evening at dusk, when we were attending a park nature lecture. Usually held in the open, on this occasion, there being a chill breeze coming down off the Rockies, we were gathered in the communal camp kitchen... a long, log-built shelter containing tables, benches and a big wood-burning range for the benefit of people travelling without cooking facilities. The naturalist had tipped a load of logs into the stove, there was coffee brewing in a couple of pots on top, we'd just watched a film about Bighorn sheep and the conversation, as usual, had turned to bears. It always did, whatever the programmed subject for the evening.

Every park naturalist had had his own bear adventures and his audience invariably wanted to hear them. In this case the naturalist, chased by a grizzly one day when he was exploring the back-country at Waterton, had taken refuge up a tree and the bear had shaken the tree-trunk in a rage. Grizzlies are known to do this on occasion: they are said to be able to tear a moderate-sized tree down. This tree withstood the battering, however, and eventually the bear made off. Rather more quickly, actually, than the naturalist had expected so, having been taught to be cautious, he stayed on up there for a while. Which was just as well because in a very short time the grizzly came back. This time accompanied by a second grizzly, said the naturalist, and they *both* tried to shake the tree down!

He was answering the usual spate of rapturous enquiries... how *had* he got down, had the bears chased him, what would he have done if they'd demolished the tree... when there was a sudden crashing of branches in the dusk outside. Quick as a flash the naturalist was at the door, and had come back and picked up one of the stove logs. Nobody rushed to follow him because everybody thought it was a bear... attracted by the smell of the coffee, and the naturalist would best know how to deal with him.

'Scat! Gerrof!' he shouted, hurling the log into the twilight, and there was a flurried crashing away into the forest that everybody listened to with relief. Except us, when the naturalist came back in and said it was that blasted moose again. Charles and I, hard though we had searched, hadn't yet seen a moose.

# Nine

WHEN WE DID SEE one it was quite by chance and so close that, looking back, I wonder why on earth we were mad enough to take photographs, but at least it proves that it happened.

We'd seen elk, we'd seen mule deer and Bighorn sheep, we'd seen black bears till we'd just about lost count of them, and a golden eagle, spotted by Charles through binoculars, on a crag above Emerald Lake. We had also, in search of moose, waited for hours by salt-licks, been bitten by mosquitoes at boggy lake-ends, lurked behind trees in various parts of forests we were assured they fed in – and still hadn't managed to see one.

Not that I imagined it would be a very exciting experience. A moose, from what I'd seen in photographs, was simply a big, ungainly type of deer. So ugly, with its football nose, as to look like a caricature. So plentiful, from what I'd read, that it populated the country like cattle. Only the fact that

we hadn't seen one made the sighting of it important...
until the memorable day when we did.

We had covered a lot of ground by this time. Been into
British Columbia and out again. Crossed the Great Divide
and the Kicking Horse River and walked, in the wake of
history, the stretch of railway track that sweeps like a sleigh-
run down the rocky slopes of the Big Hill. So often we'd
sung 'The run-away train ran down the hill and she blew,
she blew,' without for a moment realising that it was about
a real train on a mountainside in British Columbia and that
one day we would stand on the track where it happened
and see the overturned engine below. One of the engines,
anyway. Apparently it had happened quite often.

Back in the 1880s, when the Canadian Pacific Railway
was being laid across Canada, the engineers discovered
lead zinc in the rock in the Kicking Horse Pass. Lead
zinc, used in the manufacture of brass, was a very valuable
commodity and a big mining camp sprang up there.
Together with the railwaymen's camp it became one of
the frontier communities one reads of – reckless, tough, a
world completely without women, whose occupants spent
their pay on drink and gambling.

Life was so cheap they gambled even on that. Whether
the man who'd quit last week had set off the last lot of
dynamite he'd put in before he finished. Whether the one
succeeding him today was likely to hammer a spike straight
into it if he hadn't. Whether a driver bringing a train down
the hill could stop it if it ran away. And, the favourite wager
among the drivers themselves, how far they could get up
the hill without refuelling.

Superseded now by a spiral tunnel cut inside the
mountain, the Big Hill was one of the most dangerous

stretches of track in the West. It was so steep there were three run-offs from the main track for the driver to use in an emergency. If the train came down too fast and his single hand-brake wouldn't hold it, he attempted to turn the train on to one of the run-offs, the points to which were always kept open with a man on duty to watch them. If the man judged the train was under control he closed the points and it went down the hill. If not, he left them open and the driver swerved off along a run-off. If the train was going really fast the run-off wasn't much help in stopping it – the engine just rocked along it and derailed itself en route. But, as a local historian explained to us, 'It kept 'em from muckin' up the main track.'

He it was who showed us the rusted engine, still with its tall nineties funnel and the remains of its wooden cowcatcher, among the weeds at the bottom of the bank down which it had plunged. He it was who showed us the huge rock further back... split completely in two where yet another runaway engine had shot off the track and hit it, the scorch marks and oil stains still visible. He it was, too, who told us the story which never got into song, of the driver who took his engine *up* the hill in the most daring wager of them all.

Betting he would get to the top without stopping – nobody had ever made it more than half-way up – he got up steam, screwed the escape valves down tightly... normally, the higher the steam-head rose the further one opened them up for safety... took another bet or two and set the engine at the hill.

'How far did he get?' I asked. 'Further than he expected,' was the reply. 'Halfway up, the whole damned thing blew up. All they found was his gold watch, and that was three miles away.'

This of course was before there were any passenger trains through the Rockies – back in the days when the line was being laid and these were the narrow-gauge engines they used in its construction. Even so, later there were several mining train accidents on the Big Hill and in 1905 they started the spiral tunnel through the mountain. It was finished in 1910 and it takes a train four minutes to traverse it, whistling an eerie warning as it goes. One of the most nostalgic sounds of Western Canada is of a train whistling its way through the Kicking Horse Pass. Charles remembers it still from when he was six years old, going from New Brunswick to visit his aunt in Vancouver.

We tape-recorded the whistle, found ourselves a rock-boring by way of a memento – a plug of polished limestone, like a stick of sea-side rock in marble, drilled out by miners making holes to put the dynamite in... and, our heads filled with thoughts of runaway trains, the poems of Robert Service and in Charles's case the days when he was six, came back over the Kicking Horse River (so called because the man who named it was kicked into it by his horse), into Alberta, and almost immediately met up with a moose.

Just like that. 'Always stop if you see a line of cars pulled up on the roadside ahead of you,' a naturalist had told us back in Jasper. 'It means somebody has seen something interesting.'

So when we saw three cars halted on the shoulder of the road to Banff, Charles slowed the camper and, while he was manoeuvring it into a safe position (it not being our vehicle he was very careful always where he parked it), I was out, armed with the camera, tiptoeing at top speed into the trees. I don't know what I expected to see. Certainly not a bear – people would have been in their cars and all the cars were empty. A deer perhaps? A mother with a pair of spotted fawns? Out on the range one would never get near them, but they weren't nearly so nervous in the parks.

Neither was the huge buck moose who, as I stepped round my second fir tree in, stood there in the clearing before me. Ugly indeed! Sleek, shining black, a good seventeen hands high and with hindquarters as slender as a racehorse, a moose is absolutely beautiful! Outside the park, a moose would have fled at once. Inside it too, for the most part. But this one, obviously intelligent enough to have realised that in this place people only looked at him, stayed where he was and went on feeding.

He let me photograph him, taking no notice of the camera's click; moving unconcernedly, like the monarch he was, through the grass. Charles, coming up behind me having safely parked the camper, whispered 'For Pete's sake what are you doing this close! You know you've been told they're dangerous!' And then, looking at the moose, posed now like a painting by Landseer – 'Quick! We must have one like that! Let me have the camera!'

That was all right. So, as far as the moose was concerned, were the three or four other people who were now approaching cautiously through the trees, cameras raised to eye-level. We had been lucky. Stopping where Charles had done, I'd cut straight down through the trees and come upon the moose while the others were still creeping in at an angle. Very lucky, because out in front of the still photographers came crouching a little fat man with a movie camera and when the moose heard that contraption whirring towards him, he moved away with leisurely dignity.

The little fat man went after him. The moose moved off again. The little fat man followed up, whirring ecstatically at about ten feet distant. 'Lucky that's a tame moose,' said one of the more cautious ordinary photographers. 'Boy, would Fatso have to run!'

Only of course it wasn't a tame moose, just an unusually tolerant one. After a little more retreating it got fed up, lowered its antlers and charged – and Fatso did have to run. I can see him now, in a red-checked shirt and shorts, his camera accessories flying straight out on their straps behind him, streaking through the trees like a scene from a Mack Sennett film with the moose going head-down after him.

Fortunately for him it was still in an amiable mood – it just saw him off at a half-run, like a horse with a dog that has been pestering it. Then, with the man wedged deservedly up in a tree-fork, the moose moved unhurriedly off into the forest. The great black shadow became fainter among the trees until at last we were looking at nothing. 'I wish we'd had a movie camera to take that fat man running,' I said. 'Gosh,' said Charles ecstatically. 'But what a moose we've seen!'

We saw several after that. Always at a distance though, in bogs or lakeside clearings. Never such a magnificent specimen and never again at such fantastically close range. It was just about a chance in a million.

Like the time we saw the wolverine. That, however was still ahead of us. Meanwhile our yellow and white camper with the prairie rose emblem of Alberta on its registration plate took us, with only an occasional emergency stop as one of the cupboard doors swung open in the living section behind us and either the saucepans fell out at the bottom or our canned food fell out at the top (that was the only fault we could find with the camper; its door fastenings were a bit hit-or-miss)... down to Banff, along the beautiful Bow River to Calgary, south down what was once the old Fort Macleod trail, and then abruptly west, into the foothills of the Rockies.

We were on familiar ground now. Here was the spot where, on our last visit, we'd stopped to look at the rangeland in the moonlight and a coyote had come out on to the trail ahead of us. There ahead of us, at the junction of several tracks, was the little white clapboard schoolhouse... not in a village street, as one would expect a schoolhouse to be, but all by itself on the range.

The school bell still hung there, silent in its white wooden steeple, and inside was the big round wood-stove that used to warm the communal schoolroom in winter. So many children must have learned their lessons there, just above the creek with the beaver dam. So many grown-up socials and Sunday prayer-meetings it must have seen, before there was anything but horse transport into the nearest town. Unused now for years, the ranchers preserved it out of affection.

Over the wooden bridge across the creek we drove up past a white signpost giving the direction to various ranches. Somebody had peppered it with bullet-holes for fun, to add a Western flavour. We took the left-hand fork. We were going to the Ewings' ranch. On, it seemed endlessly, along a rough, red-dust track, our way blocked at intervals by wandering cattle – our friend Sherm Ewing's herd of Herefords, spread like a milling sea across the rangeland. At last we drove through the great log gate that closed off the home corral, down to the ranch-house nestling in the bowl of the valley, and Claire Ewing, slim in Western jeans, was coming out to meet us. It was as if we had come home.

In more ways than one. We had spent a lot of time here on our first trip and every corner of the place was familiar. Its setting, too, was very like our own at home. The rolling hills made for galloping, the pine forest darkening the head of the valley – except that this, of course, was on a much bigger scale and there were the snow-covered Rockies in the background. There were cats at the ranch and the dog. Sage, who remembered us. The only thing missing, we said laughingly, was Annabel. Then Sherm and his son Charlie appeared, doffing their Stetsons, clattering in off the verandah in their high-heeled Western boots. 'We knew you were here, by the camper in the yard,' said Sherm. 'So we stopped off and did a bit of saddling up. We thought you might like a ride before supper. You'll find a couple of your friends at the door.'

There she was when we went out. Sheba, the part-Arab cow pony I'd ridden two years before. She still had the barrel-shaped stomach that any other Arab would have been ashamed of, but which she found so useful when she decided to slip her cinch. I'd ridden miles lopsided on that wilful little pony because, however much one tightened it, her saddle kept sliding round. Uphill, downhill, Sheba deciding the direction, while I concentrated, sweating, on staying on.

'Not this time, my beauty,' I told her, thinking of the practice I'd put in for this on Mio, riding up the precipitous Slagger's Path at home standing up with my arms outstretched, fast-trotting down the lane on the way back to the stables, arms folded, deliberately without reins...

Sheba regarded me with an Annabel look from beneath her dark Arab eyelashes, then snorted and rubbed her nose against Biz, the big roan who was tethered alongside her.

'Here they are again.' You could practically hear her saying it. 'What shall we do with them this time? You like to have first try?'

That, at any rate, is the only reason I can give for the fact that when Charles put his foot to Biz's stirrup. Biz, who'd behaved last time as if he were Olympia trained and Charles the rangeland Alan Oliver, stood up on his hind legs, waved his front ones, and started to panic backwards.

Charles, clinging to him like a leech for a second or two, got his other leg over the saddle. Biz came down from his rearing, and Charles leaned forward to pat him. Up went Biz again... backing, with Charles in the saddle, straight for the open barn door while Sheba looked approvingly on. 'Wait till this one gets on *me*,' said the semaphore tilt of her eartips. 'I'll come in backwards too. It'll look just like we're ballet dancing... or one of those funny films they run in reverse.'

It no doubt would have done too, except that Charles is a pretty good horseman and Biz suddenly found himself going forward against his will, whereat Sheba, seeing him walk submissively across the yard, let me get up on her and followed after him.

'Where are we going to have the fun then? Up on the hill?' was the undoubted meaning of her second snort. I rode out as if I'd been a cowgirl all my life – but oh boy! did I wish I was walking!

## Ten

BIZ, ONCE HE WAS out of the yard, was perfectly all right. He'd got this habit lately, said Sherm, of playing up when people got on him. Seemed to have got a ticklish back. He'd bucked Charlie clean off the other day.

I looked surreptitiously at Charles. This was what happened when you rode in the West. People regarded being bucked or reared with as natural, like crossing the road. Apparently Charles regarded it that way too. He beamed back at me, reins loose on Biz's neck, as if he rode perpendicular horses practically every day.

Not so me. I manoeuvred Sheba behind Biz and Sherm's horse, Duke, with every intention of keeping her there. Biz's capers had unnerved me. Just let Sheba get the chance... I remembered her speed from last time. She trudged there for a while, obviously insulted, her head down like Annabel's when she, too, was being a Slave in Bondage. Her shoulders moved wearily. Her head drooped lower. She must stop for a Moment, she said. She wasn't as young as she used to be and I was quite a weight to carry.

I let her rest. We were climbing the steep hill opposite the ranch-house: she couldn't do anything very disastrous on that gradient. Even though, when she did plod on again, we were quite a way behind Sherm and Charles. By the time she'd stopped for another couple of breathers we were even further behind. The track was narrow and sunken, though. There were bushes on either side. And ahead of us the hefty rumps of Biz and Duke blocked our way like a wall of sandbags.

At the top of the path she paused again, turning her head very quietly to the left. One of her little tricks, I thought, tightening up the reins. I bet there was a sidepath round here and she had some idea of taking it. But no, when I followed the pointing of her ears, it was to see a mule deer watching us from about twenty yards away, its head and shoulders above a bush. The pair of them regarded each other silently for a while, then Sheba resumed her upward trudge. How was that for observation? said her ears, now tilted back at me. That old Biz and Duke hadn't seen that one.

They hadn't, as a result of which they were now several hundred yards ahead of us, ambling placidly side by side as their riders chatted. Gosh, we were all Behind! said Sheba, suddenly quickening her pace. We were still on the narrow track, so I let her. But, as she was obviously aware, knowing these paths like the palm of her hoof, by the time we caught up with the others, the narrow trail had ended. We were out on the wide, open top of the hill now and we went round Biz and Duke like a racing car round a bollard.

'The West gets her like this,' I heard Charles say as I shot past. 'She's been looking forward to a good long gallop for weeks.' Not like this I hadn't, apparently bound straight for the border, with nobody in front to block my path. Sherm and Charles, I knew, would have come tearing after me, but pride wouldn't let me yell for help. I was supposed to be able to *ride*!

We flew along the hilltop, clearing scrub bushes and gopher holes as we went. I expected to go down at any moment. But we didn't. Sheba was a cow-pony, used to ground like this. She knew what she was doing. And then the thought came to me – what on earth was I worrying about? I'd never come off yet on Mio. If Sheba was safe on her feet- and she seemed to be – I ought to be enjoying it.

'Sit down! Get your hands down! Work alternately on the reins!' I could hear Mrs Hutchings saying it. I did. Sheba was still going like a catapult along the hilltop but I began to feel her responding. I slowed her pace down... gently... not wanting to turn her head so she couldn't see where she was going over the gopher holes. I had her. We were back now to a rhythmic, loping canter. I could watch the way ahead, avoid the holes. And suddenly it was glorious... exhilarating... the thud of her hooves on the turf, the wide Canadian sky, the rolling rangeland, the feeling of boundlessness... 'Enjoying it?' asked Sherm, as he and Charles caught me up. 'You bet,' I said, patting my trusty steed's neck. 'She really is a good girl.'

Except, of course, that she'd managed to loosen her cinch and it was no good Sherm tightening it up. Cutting steeply down the hillside at the head of the valley she got it loose again and both the saddle and I went sideways. Taking advantage of this, Sheba started to get up speed again, obviously intending to nip down and get past the others. She thought I liked it out in front, she said when I pulled her up. She just wanted to show me how she could go Downhill.

I'd take her word for it, I said, bringing her back behind Biz and Duke and putting her nose once more into their tails. I'd ride her flat out anywhere now, so long as we were on a reasonable level – but not with her saddle canted 40 degrees to starboard, going downhill on a slope like Ben Nevis.

Two happy days we spent riding the range again, the camper parked by the side of the ranch-house, but we had to get on to see those grizzlies. Regretfully we said goodbye to the Ewings, told Biz and Duke we'd be back one day, and set out for a neighbouring valley. Here, at the Box X Ranch, lived another of our friends. Babe Burton. A splendid trout stream waters her land and there are several beaver dams in it. But we were not going fishing or watching beavers at work this time. We were on our way to Waterton and she was coming with us. As far as her cabin at Yarrow Creek, anyway, a couple of miles from the Waterton Park boundary. There we really would be in grizzly country.

When we set out in our respective vehicles to drive the forty miles from the Box X to the cabin, Babe carried a high-powered rifle in her truck. Not because she was nervous. She knew the wilderness and its animals better than most people. But there could always come a time when she might need it. She'd have felt safer, no doubt, if she'd had it along the time she was caught between a grizzly and her cubs.

For many years, the grizzlies around Yarrow Creek had a reputation for being exceptionally aggressive – the result, it was said, of an incident back in the 1860s, when a band of Indians who were camped there developed smallpox. Indians took smallpox very badly indeed – whole encampments would be wiped out in no time – and while the band lay in their teepees along the creek bank, too sick to bury their dead, grizzlies, attracted by the smell, had come padding into the camp. They had begun to feed on the dead bodies, had gone on to pull the living out of their tents most of them were too weak to resist; only a few survivors got away. From then on Yarrow Canyon was taboo: no Indian ever entered it again. When some forty years later, Babe's father decided to build a cabin there, the Indians did their best to dissuade him. It was full of ghosts, they said.

And, presumably, grizzly bears. There were still an unusually large number around and they had a reputation for deliberately attacking people. They were believed to have acquired a taste for human flesh and, with the memory of non-resistance in the teepees, to have lost their fear of humans. It could have been so. A grizzly can live to be 40 and their non-fear could have been passed on to their descendants. Gradually the trait had faded, however, and the story of how it started. Nowadays probably few people in the Yarrow district ever think of it. Except on such an occasion as when Babe got caught between the bears.

It seemed that one of her neighbours had a cow which had been ailing for quite a while. The owner dosed it with all kinds of remedies and when the cow eventually died... a couple of hundred yards from Babe's boundary fence: she could see it from her window... he hadn't bothered about moving it because there was no value in the carcass.

Inevitably the grizzlies arrived – a large male, a medium male, a female and her half-grown cubs. They fed always in that order. Woe betide a lesser bear that tried to eat before its superior. In the normal way, said Babe, they'd have eaten the cow in no time, but with all that medicine in it, obviously it hadn't tasted so good. They'd chew at it, go off again... they came every day for about three weeks. The males then disappeared, there being little left of the cow – but the mother still came with her cubs, so they could play at attacking and practise fighting with the bones.

Babe had watched many bears in her time, but none so consistently as these. The cubs, she said, were some two years old and seemed to be always squabbling. The mother would stand it for a while, then she'd lose her patience, grow irritable and hit them. A hefty cuff that sent them reeling and they'd hide in the bushes and cry like children for a while. Then out they'd come, bouncing after Mum, a new leaf definitely turned – until they forgot, and started to quarrel, and their mother would whack them again. She was obviously fed up with them. It was nearly time for them to be going off on their own, and for her to think of re-mating, which she couldn't do while she still had cubs around because a male bear would have killed them. But still they trailed persistently after her – and of course she would have defended them with her life. It was just that she wanted them to start being independent, not forever quarrelling and harrassing her.

Babe, all this time, had carried on as usual. Even when there'd been five bears feeding just over the boundary fence she'd gone out to her truck, brought in wood, fetched greens in from the garden. They weren't interested in her, she said. They'd probably watched her often at the cabin and knew that she presented no danger. All she did make sure of, when she went out into the open, was that the mother and cubs were together.

Until one day she was hoeing the vegetable patch down at the creek-side, thinking the bears were nowhere around, and suddenly she heard the cubs crying and when she looked up, they were on top of the bank on her right... bawling like mad for Mum who, to Babe's horror, suddenly appeared across the creek on her left. She had nothing but the hoe to defend herself with. She thought she hadn't a chance. And then, she said, the she-bear looked at her... looked beyond her at the cubs... and deliberately turned back into the woods leaving them to their own devices. It obviously knew Babe wouldn't harm the cubs and as for her trying to steal them (which is apparently a continual fear with mother bears)... this one was patently so fed up with those two that if Babe wanted them, she was welcome!

Another time at Yarrow Creek Babe had actually seen a stolen cub. Apparently bears have a tremendously strong maternal instinct and, even while they have young themselves, if they can get another bear's cubs away from her they will – fighting her for their possession if necessary, and adding them to their own litter. Unfortunately the instinct stops at that. They never treat the stolen cubs as well as they do their own, acting towards them like Cinderella's stepmother. You could always tell a stolen cub, said Babe, from the fact that it would be thinner and poorer-looking than the others.

So when this particular procession passed through the Canyon one day... a female grizzly, two sturdy, playful cubs and a third one crying and dawdling in the rear... it didn't need much deduction to work out that the third cub had been abducted. It was tatty-looking and seemed to be trying to get left behind. Probably its real mother was still following it through the woods. But every now and then back would come its new mother, growling and cuffing it for being tardy. And on would hurry the little bear, crying more loudly still.

If she could have done anything to help it she would have, said Babe. She was watching from a track higher up. But if she'd shouted or thrown a stone the she-bear would have attacked her, with such very young cubs in question. So the procession had passed on... down into a steep gully and up again, the twins following happily on the heels of their mother, the third one dropping once more behind. Evidently he thought the gully was a good place to get lost in – but alas, he hadn't a chance. Back came the she-bear to stand impatiently on the rim and tell him what would happen to him if he didn't hurry... which he obviously decided he'd better do, but, having lagged behind while the others had climbed out, he couldn't find the way out of the gully. He panicked, said Babe... kept scrambling up and falling down again, till at last he got up and over the top in sheer terror. The she-bear hit him, he fled down the path with her growling after him, and that was the last Babe saw of the group. She'd heard a crackling in the woods a while later, though, and hoped his real mother was still following.

That had been quite an experience, but Babe had had plenty, living all her life in the Rockies. Once, bird-watching up in the hills, she had come across an enormous hole under a rock... and beat it fast when she realised it was a bear-den, with signs that the bear had been recently working on it. And once – she talked of them still with great affection – she had looked after a pair of grizzly cubs.

This was back in the days when her husband was alive and they were acting as guides to a surveying party. A bear kept stealing meat from the cook-tent, which was just behind the tent they slept in and her husband, hearing a movement one night, had raised their back tent-flap to see the huge, steel-hooked feet right in front of him. He had shot the bear... it was coming every night and was a danger... not realising that it was a female. Or, until they heard piteous crying next day from the slope beyond the camp, that she had a pair of cubs. She must have left them hidden in the bushes while she made her raid and they were still waiting for her to come back. Calling anxiously down at the camp because they knew that was where she had gone, but afraid to venture from the spot where she'd put them because small bears are trained to be obedient.

They put food out for them, said Babe. They felt terrible at having killed the mother: at the time they'd only thought of the danger. The cubs had cautiously taken the food and after a few days had ventured into camp, and, because they were obviously lonely as well as hungry, she'd taken on the job of looking after them. They went off every night... after a week of searching she found where they were sleeping. Across a scree of rock under some pine trees, obviously the last place they'd slept with their mother. But every day they lolloped down into camp... a roly-poly male and a little female. The male was the world's extrovert, always investigating something, but his sister was a small and nervous-looking and she obviously worried a lot about him. 'Roff!' she would call. 'Roff! roff!' when she thought he was doing something he shouldn't... pulling blankets and towels off the airing-line or sticking his head into some-body's tent. So they called him Ralph and he answered to it, though they'd never given the girl a name.

The horses were very curious and were always snorting round them... normally they would rear and whinny at the scent of a bear, but the cubs had obviously acquired the smell of the camp and the horses couldn't make it out. One day, said Babe, she left her soap on a rock, and as soon as her back was turned Ralph stole it. She heard a gurgling noise... turned to see Ralph snuggling the Lifebuoy in his paws and rolling with it clasped to him, a sign that he was happy... and then up came two mules and started sniffing at him. She never knew what he'd have done with the soap. He dropped it and ran for his life!

They grew to trust her. They would come when she called and they'd take bread with bacon grease and honey – their favourite food – from her hands. Another week, she said, and she would have been able to touch them, but her father was ill and she had to leave camp to go and see him. While she was packing in her tent she heard the she-cub calling 'Roff! roff!' outside and knew that the male must be up to something, so she pulled back the flap – and his nose was right there. He'd been lying on his stomach watching her.

The cubs had followed her a long way up the trail when she rode out. It was the first time they'd known her go away. She could see them now as they were when she looked back, she said... two small, forlorn figures looking after her. She was away for three weeks, and when she came back they had gone. Her husband said they'd stayed waiting for her at the top of the trail for days. He'd put food up there for them, but they wouldn't come to him, and finally they'd disappeared.

It was just as well, said Babe. They'd eventually have had to go to a zoo. She couldn't have kept them when they grew bigger, and half-tamed animals in the wild were sitting targets for hunters. But she'd never forget the magic of having been, for a short while, the friend of two small grizzly bears.

# Eleven

BABE'S BROTHER-IN-LAW is Andy Russell, author of *Grizzly Country*, who lives a few miles from Yarrow Creek in a rambling, log-built ranch-house high up on the edge of the Rockies.

Andy, one of Canada's most ardent conservationists, is considered to be the foremost non-scientific authority on the grizzly, whom he has known as a hunter and mountain guide, and now as a naturalist and photographer, all his life. It was one of the highlights of our trip to meet him and we cared nothing for the frantic falling out of the pots and pans from the cupboards in the back of the camper as we drove to the Hawk's Nest up a rough, winding dirt road that eventually resolved itself into a washed-out rock gully, bordered on either side by bushes loaded with ripening saskatoon berries. You could pick buckets and buckets of them up here for bottling, said Babe – she and her sister Kay, Andy's wife, often did – and still there'd be plenty for the bears. 'Actually on this track up to the ranch?' we asked. 'Goodness yes,' she said. 'They often see grizzlies up here.'

They did too. Andy has expeditioned, in his study of the grizzly, from Montana as far north as the Yukon and Alaska, but some of his most interesting experiences have been on his own home ground. We sat in front of the log fire in the great ranch fireplace till the early hours of the morning, listening to some of them.

To the tale, for instance, of how his car had stuck one wet night in a pothole in the gully we'd come up. Unable to move it, he'd left it and was walking the last half-mile up to the ranch when, rounding a bend in the track, he heard an unmistakable growl right by the side of him. Unable to see – he hadn't a torch – all he could do was stand still... the thing bear experts advocate when there is no other way out, but it takes considerable strength of mind to do it. For what seemed ages he stood like a stone while the unseen bear, annoyed at being surprised, rambled and ranted about people Creeping Up on him and what, for two pins, he'd do. At last, having said his piece, the bear crashed away into the trees behind him and Andy walked, sweating, on up to the ranch. How close he'd been he learned next day when he and his son went down to haul out the car. The tracks of a big grizzly, clear in the damp earth, ended six paces from where Andy had been standing.

The story I liked best, though, was of the grizzly that was fascinated by their cat, and had tolerated their terrier's barking and charging at him as a sheepdog would do with a puppy. This was extraordinary in itself. Most bears would have attacked the dog on sight. Undoubtedly, as with Babe and the bears at her cabin, the Hawk's Nest grizzlies sensed that the humans there meant no harm to them, neither did their animals, and so they were content to browse around in a state of mutual toleration. Except when clumsy clots frightened the daylights out of them in the dark, of course, and had to be taught a lesson.

This particular bear had first appeared as a teenage cub, accompanying his mother and brother. The trio had been around in the vicinity of the ranch for weeks, feeding on a dead horse. They bothered nobody, but several times came quite close to the ranch-house, obviously interested in its occupants. One night, indeed, the Russells, hearing a noise, switched on the porch-light and found the she-bear right outside the door.

She became too confident, however, and one night she went over to a neighbour's ranch and started looking into a truck that was parked in the yard. The rancher, roused by his dog barking, came out and took a shot at her. She made off, wounded. Fortunately her injuries were only slight, but she had learned her lesson about humans. Shortly afterwards she and one of the cubs left the district. So, presumably hearing of the incident did various other grizzlies that had been around. None were seen in the area for ages – except for the second cub who, being now almost adult, had been living for a while on his own, and who some time later started appearing around the ranch-house, as if there was somebody or something that attracted him.

The Russells discovered it was their cat, who had considerable spunk. When the grizzly appeared the cat, instead of running, would raise its back and threaten to pulverise its adversary, while the bear, its head on one side, stood studying it, completely fascinated. One day they found the cat howling its threats on the doorstep and the bear with its head through the porch door, making no attempt to touch the screamer. Just obviously puzzling how on earth it *made* a noise like that.

All this time the terrier was barking and rushing at the bear, who took no notice of him at all, as if he knew it was part of the Hawk's Nest set-up and one just had to put up with these things. The young grizzly came again and again to the ranch-house and by late summer the position was such that when Kay, Andy's wife, was picking saskatoons in the gully, the bear often appeared eating berries in the same patch. Never coming close enough to be embarrassing but obviously liking to be – like Annabel grazing on the other side of the fence when we're gardening at home – eating in company. With the terrier forever barking around him and the grizzly amiably taking no notice.

It was a marvellous story. So were the many others Andy told us and we'd have given anything to have seen one of the Hawk's Nest bears, but there were none around right then. The berry season had started and the bears were down in the lower valleys eating them. It would be a week or two yet before they ripened up here and one might see a grizzly stripping them happily with his claws, and we had to get on to Glacier: we had only two weeks left of our trip. So we said goodbye to the Russells, and to Babe who had to get back to her ranch, and drove on down to Waterton Park and our meeting with the wolverine.

Andy, writing to us later, said the little red gods of the wilds must have been with us on that trip. He had seen only three wolverines in his life – most Canadians have never seen one – and we had to walk straight into one on a trail above Cameron Lake.

We were up there, needless to say, looking for a grizzly. We'd stopped at the lake in the early afternoon and when we saw the notice up in the campground saying one had been reported on the Alderson trail... 'At last,' we said and were off up the Alderson trail like rockets, though that was hardly the intention of the notice, which warned people that they travelled it at their own risk.

We'd walk as far as we could in three hours, we decided, then we'd have to turn and come back. It would be dusk by the time we got back to the campsite, but that would serve our purpose very well. By then the other walkers would be mostly down off the trail (always supposing, after that notice, there were any on it) and late evening, on a path undisturbed by clattering hikers, was when we might catch a wandering grizzly unawares.

So we said when we set out from Cameron but after a while I wondered whether it had been such a good idea. It was a sweltering afternoon and the track wove relentlessly up-wards, snaking back and forth on itself in long switchback bends. After an hour we could still see Cameron Lake below us, and the ridge above seemed as far away as ever. Then we realised we were going round the side of the mountain as we climbed, not over it, and the lake disappeared from view, and we emerged from deep forest on to a high mountain plateau, dotted with granite crags and occasional stunted pines. Many of them had been struck by lightning and the dead brown huddles of their lower branches looked, at first glance and at a distance, as if a bear was standing under them watching us.

'Always look for a tree in case you need it'... I remembered the oft-repeated warning, and my progress along the track behind Charles at that stage was accompanied by rapid mental calculations. How far was it to the tree over there... and if I went up that sloping branch... the one that drooped down to the ground so conveniently... could a bear get up it as well? Or would it be better to take a jump at a tree with no lower branches... and what would happen if I missed?

Which is not to say I regretted being there. I longed to see a grizzly. It was just the feeling, out in the open, of being vulnerable, in No Man's Land.

Halfway across the plateau we were caught by a thunderstorm and had to shelter under one of the pine trees. The thunder rolled, lightning hissed from peak to peak around us like the striking of angry giant snakes: I had never heard it hiss before: I supposed it was being so near to the peaks. Hailstones slashed down like bullets, ricochetting viciously off the rocks and ground. All it needed now, I decided, was for the grizzly to come along, annoyed at being hit by the hailstones, and see us and blame us for doing it. We wouldn't get very far up this stunted tree. I imagined him sniffing at our dangling heels... But the thunderstorm passed and the sun came out brilliantly again, raising steam from the pathway and melting the huddles of hail-stones, and on we trudged to Summit Lake, then up again on more of those switchbacks... above timberline now, crossing vivid red scree, with a view of the icefields beyond Mount Custer. We got as far as Carthew Pass – we could see the two Carthew Lakes far below us – and there we had to turn back. Our three hours were up. It was too late to go any further. And still we hadn't seen our grizzly.

We hadn't seen anything. Not even a mountain goat. It had all been a waste of effort. Or had it... when we looked across at the icefields, and remembered the lightning playing around the mountains, and the effect of the sun coming out after the storm?

We made faster time going downhill. We were only half an hour from Cameron Lake when I rounded a switchback bend ahead of Charles and saw an animal on the track. A grey animal, with a head like a fox but with a longer-textured coat, more like a badger's, sitting on the path in a patch of the orange evening sun which filtered low through the forest branches. I put a hand behind me to halt Charles and we stood there as silent as shadows. For a moment, then the animal saw us and was away up the bank with a gliding motion. Its legs seemed short, but it had a brush like a fox, and I have never seen an animal move so fast.

'A grey fox' said our neighbours at the campsite when we told them – and that was what we thought ourselves. Until we described it to the Cameron Lake naturalist that night and he told us we'd seen a wolverine. He'd never seen one himself, he said – only a stuffed one in a museum. They were one of the rarest, shyest animals in Canada... brother! had we had the luck!

It was the fiercest animal for its size in North America, he told us; the only one ever known to stand up to a grizzly. A grizzly could kill it with one swat of its paw but it had to make contact first, and with the speed and temper and teeth of the wolverine, the grizzly usually thought twice. It was really a fox-sized weasel, said the naturalist... that would give us some indication. No, it wouldn't attack humans. It was far too elusive, which was why people so rarely saw it. Probably the thunderstorm had achieved it for us. The wolverine had most likely been caught in it, got its long coat wet, and was sitting in the patch of sun to dry out. Brother! repeated the naturalist enviously. He'd seen plenty of grizzlies, but to have seen a wolverine!

In the end we saw our grizzly as well, but not until our final week. In the Granite Park area, which was where I'd all along banked on finding one, and with all the more sense of achievement because the previous night I'd got cold feet.

Quite literally. Our camper was parked at Apgar on Lake Macdonald... not all that far, as the crow flew, from Trout Lake where one of the girls had been killed, and for all that we were in a proper campsite there were plenty of bears around. The ranger had been telling us only that evening of the silly things some people did... like a few weeks back when some hikers had gone into a roped-off section of the campsite and slept in the open in sleeping bags.

The area had been roped off to allow trodden-down vegetation to recover and nobody had camped there for weeks. The hikers had slipped in there to avoid paying camp fees, not realising that bears were going through it at night. One of the boys, who had ginger hair, had been roused by a blow on the head. Fortunately it was a black bear. They thought he'd mistaken the red hair for a marmot. He'd taken a swipe and had run like mad when he heard the screams. The boy had had to have his scalp stitched but was otherwise unharmed. Had the blow come from a grizzly, it would have killed him.

What with hearing about that, and my bedtime reading of *Night of the Grizzlies* – we were now in Glacier Park where it had happened – it was small wonder that I woke around three in the morning, with a distinct feeling that there were bears around and a consciousness of being very cold. Clear white moonlight was shining through the camper windows and I realised that Charles, too, was awake. 'Brrr... it's cold in here,' he said. And then, sitting up – 'Great Scott! The door's wide open!'

It was too. One of those temperamental locks again and presumably we hadn't fastened it properly. But how had it come as wide open as that with the camper completely stationary? Had something clawed or nosed at it? I expected to see a hump-backed head at any moment. Charles shot out of bed, grabbed the door and pulled it shut. 'It's all right now,' he said. But was it? Supposing the door came open again when we were asleep and there *was* a bear outside... and it came in and there we were with no escape way through to the front?

I lay awake for the remainder of the night asking myself why I never learned... what was I doing getting mixed up with bears when I could be snug in our little valley at home? A question I asked myself even more emphatically next morning, on a cliff face high above the Logan Pass.

This, we'd read, was the best way in to Granite Park. To leave the camper at the top of the Pass on the Going-to-the-Sun Highway and walk the seven-mile Highline Trail. 'It invades the haunts of mountain goats, big-horns and cougars,' said the guide book, 'and is above timberline throughout its length.' It mentioned also an alpine meadow studded with glacier lilies and gentians and that further on there were slopes of the spectacular bear-grass; tall, with upright plumes, like a sea of cream-coloured red-hot pokers; so far we'd only seen it in photographs. Bears and deer frequented the slopes on hot days, it said, to escape the torment of the insects lower down... adding as if anything more were needed, that 'nutcrackers, eagles and mountain-loving birds make this their airy home'.

Carried away by that picture I overlooked the bit where it said that the trail was gouged in part out of the sheer cliff... until I was actually on it, clinging like a limpet to the back of Charles's belt, with my legs turned to half-set jelly and Charles telling me not to look down.

This was right at the beginning – where, striking off from the road at the top of the Pass, the trail runs immediately on a horizontal ledge around the cliff-face with the road dropping sharply away below it. For a while the trail is actually right above the road, like a gallery. How could I not look down when, every time I put a trembling foot forward, far below me was the continual, eye-catching, movement of cars negotiating the Pass?

I felt like a fly on a wall. I wished I was one. I'd have suckers on my feet. 'Would you like to go back?' asked Charles. 'I'm going to see that grizzly,' I said. So on we went and half-way along the ledge – wouldn't you have bet it – we met a girl coming towards us and I had to let go of Charles to let her pass. Charles swung round her. She swung nonchalantly round me. 'Don't you like heights?' she enquired as she passed. When I asked Charles afterwards how he thought she knew he said she didn't need to be clairvoyant. 'You looked as though you were tightrope-walking over Niagara,' he said, 'and boy, was your face green!'

I made it, though. We reached the end of the ledge at last and soon we were out on an easy mountain track. There were other steep bits ahead, but none as bad as that first one. I was glad I hadn't turned back. The trail ran level for about three miles with tremendous views to the valley below; then, passing over the saddle of Haystack Butte, it began to climb gradually upwards. We were crossing a scree slope now... under the razor edge of the Garden Wall, as they call this towering section of the Great Divide. Above us, among the rocks and scree, we could see marmots scuttling about... a prime attraction for hungry grizzlies. Below us, on our left, were odd patches of alder trees and berry bushes: there could be a bear in any of those.

We trod as quietly as possible. We scanned the downward slope through binoculars. Never a sign of a bear. Until, as we reached a spot where a small stream trickled across the path, Charles stopped suddenly and said he could smell wet dog. So could I. As if someone had given a Saint Bernard a bath... a sign that a bear had crossed the path not long before. There was a tree patch below us; the stream trickled into it; we sat on the path and watched. We saw her within minutes. A silver-tipped grizzly female. Her coat a little ragged – bears' coats are not at their best in August – but still she was magnificent, with a thick, silver-tipped ruff like a husky dog's, silver frosting on her great dark back, and the powerful humped neck that is typical of the grizzly.

She was lazily cropping the bushes. Fortunately the wind was against us and not once did she look up in our direction. We watched, scarcely able to believe it... I kept telling myself that this was real... and suddenly, as we moved, we saw two cubs close beside her. One as dark as she was, one much lighter; probably he took after his Dad. They were eating too and seemed very obedient and docile, except that when she moved they dashed with her like playful kittens. How many had experienced such a moment as this? I thought of Andy Russell's words: 'To share a mountain with a grizzly for a while is a privilege and adventure like no other.'

We watched until we heard voices in the distance and saw a party of hikers coming towards us, then we got up and strolled on casually, as if we'd been taking a rest. We hoped the hikers wouldn't look down as they passed the spot where we'd been sitting, and they didn't. They were too busy talking to one another. The bears would probably have heard them and taken cover anyway, but we didn't want people gawking and pointing at them... maybe getting scared and throwing stones to drive them away. There they were, secluded and happy on their mountain. There we let them remain.

I didn't feel so noble that afternoon, I'm afraid. It was around five o'clock and we were up at Granite Park Chalet... sitting on the terrace, looking out at the mountains, talking to other walkers who were staying up there for the night. We'd have to start back in about an hour, I commented. We had to get back to Logan Pass. Not the way we'd come, though. We were going down the Alder Trail, which was quicker, and I'd read there was a good chance of seeing a grizzly going round the steep bends.

'You're going down *tonight*?' said the naturalist who was with the walkers. 'Boy, don't you go down the Alder Trail. The bears'll be about now... it's their evening feeding time and you don't want to turn a corner into a hungry bear. If you're going, you go fast down the Loop Trail.'

We did. Provided with a tin filled with stones by the naturalist and instructions to rattle it all the way, we were on our way within minutes, watched by the walking party from the top of the track.

The Loop Trail, despite its name, is the most direct route down to the road – four miles straight down the mountainside by a rough, precipitous track. It is so called because it emerges on a spectacular loop in the highway where the road switches suddenly from north-west to south-east. It was quicker. It was straight. There was no chance of a bear being round a corner. In one way I was sorry, but the naturalist obviously knew best. The one thing that had me nervous – I knew it from reading *Night of the Grizzlies* – was that the Loop Trail ran adjacent to the campground where the girl had been killed that night, and that, while there might not be any corners for them to be around, grizzlies were known very often to use this trail.

There might not be many corners but there were an awful lot of bushes about. The sort that one could easily imagine bears behind, on the banks of the narrow, sunken trail. I rattled the tin, even while I hated doing it. What was the point of frightening the bears when we'd come specially to see them? There is a sinister air, though, about the overhung Loop Trail. On it one remembers the tragedy. So I rattled like mad, sat down several times... we were going fast and the way was precipitous... and, when we were almost at the bottom, with a foot-bridge across the stream ahead of us, a sure sign of civilization... I felt thoroughly ashamed of myself. I shouldn't have rattled. We might have seen another bear and now it was too late. There wouldn't be any down here.

We had oranges in our pockets. 'Let's sit down here and eat them,' I said, anxious for the last bit of atmosphere.

'Not till we get to the road,' said Charles. 'The smell of oranges carries.' I followed him, thinking how silly that was... a well-used footbridge here, the road only yards ahead. We crossed the bridge. There was a notice-board beyond it, carrying the usual warning to hikers about bears. At least – it had carried it. The notice had been ripped. Half of it lay on the ground, together with the pulled-off top of the board. There was a curved slash-mark down the paper– more slash-marks on the pole – and, on the ground, what could have been the droppings of a very large dog.

They weren't, of course. They were a bear's. A man in the Loop parking-ground told us. We recognised him as having been up at Granite Park and went across to talk to him. Furthermore, he said, he'd come off the trail about twenty minutes ahead of us and the notice-board had been intact then: he remembered looking at it.

So we'd narrowly missed another bear. Was it a black or a grizzly? An expert could have told from the size of the droppings, but we knew nothing about that. Only that it was one that went around clawing at notices. Maybe it was a good thing we *had* missed it... or was it just feeling bored?

Charles said he bet nobody would believe us at home – about the experiences we'd had in one day.

# Twelve

WE WENT HOME WITHIN a week and they believed us all right. Father Adams' verdict was that 'twould have served us right if we had been et. Fred Ferry said 'twas a pity I'd rattled them stones, wunnit? What he meant by that we weren't quite sure. Miss Wellington said it made her come all over giddy just to *think* of me up on that cliff ledge... After which they embarked on an account of what had happened in the village in our absence and we wondered if we hadn't been safer in Canada.

For a start, Tim Bannett had gone in for keeping bees and was talking of getting a goat, in both of which activities he was being encouraged by Miss Wellington, no doubt with thoughts of honey for tea and goats' milk cheese and herself in a flowery smock helping to sell them. They'd been looking at possible goats, the bees were already installed, and Tim was getting stung almost daily.

'Hasn't he got a veil?' asked Charles, who'd been an ardent bee-keeper himself until a number of stings built up on him and he proved to be allergic. Oh yes, replied Miss Wellington – but he wasn't getting stung actually handling the bees. He'd been reading about communicating with them and he was putting it into practice – taking siestas on a chaise longue in front of the hive where he could study them and transmit thoughts of trust and friendship as they flew in and out over his head.

One couldn't communicate trust to them wearing a bee-veil, could one? she asked. I said it didn't sound as if he was communicating much without one. These were early days yet, said Miss Wellington. Just give the dear little creatures a chance to settle in.

Father Adams contributed the next item of interest. Had we heard about Mr Duggald, he asked. He were goin' round bandaged up like a mummy, having been bitten by Fred Ferry's cousin Bill's dog.

Actually it wasn't as bad as that. It was only his hand that had been bitten. It seemed that Bill Ferry's daughter was getting married and Bill, talking about it in the pub, had said his wife was drivin' him fair nuts about who had to pay for what, which side of the church people sat on, and the flowers and all that muck. Mr Duggald had told his wife, who happened to have a book on etiquette, and she'd sent him round to Bill Ferry's with it specially... he'd said it could wait till opening-time but Mrs Duggald, trying to be neighbourly, insisted he took it round at once.

There was nobody at home when he got there, so he'd opened the door to leave the book on the kitchen table. Bill's dog was in the kitchen: Mr Duggald bent down to stroke it and the dog promptly bit him in the hand. 'Thic dog hadn't read thic book on etiquette,' said Father Adams, who thought the whole thing uproariously funny. Unlike Mr Duggald, with a tetanus injection and stitches in his hand, and Mrs Duggald feeling it was all her fault for sending him, and Bill Ferry now assiduously avoiding Mr Duggald and not speaking to him when they did meet by accident. 'In case he sues 'n' explained Father Adams, who obviously hoped that he would.

This being ground where the Ferry family no doubt thought it best to tread softly, Fred, pretended he hadn't heard that one. Had we, he asked, changing the subject, seen Ern Biggs limpin' around? When we said no, who'd bitten him, Fred said *he'd* got water on the knee. Tripped over the guard stone outside the pub wall – the one put there to stop the milk lorry knocking it down. 'Bin there for years,' Fred said expansively, 'but theest know old Ern when he's had a drop too much. Out of the door, legs weavin' like withy plaits, flat on his face over th' stone. Hobblin' around with a stick he is, and threatening he's goin' to...' He stopped, realising what he'd almost said. 'Sue 'em,' completed Father Adams.

So now we knew, when we saw Tim Bannett with an angry bump on his nose, Mr Duggald with his hand in a sling, and Ern Biggs limping along with a sag to his knees that increased when he was passing the pub. For ourselves, we fetched the cats from Halstock, and Annabel back from the farm, and settled down to the autumn, dreaming of all we had seen – with Charles worrying intermittently about our swallows, which had gone when we got back. He thought they'd have stayed till October, he said – the brood had been still quite young when we left. Maybe that was why they'd gone early, I said – to get them to Africa before the colder weather set in. Whether they'd survived, or whether something had happened to them, we wouldn't know till the following Spring – when, if we were lucky, one day they'd come back.

To this end we decided not to replace the glass in the garage window – a state of affairs that considerably worried Ern Biggs on the occasions when he came limping manfully past. 'Want I put the glass back for thee?' he enquired. 'I could manage if theest hold the ladder.' ''N then fall off and blame *that* for thee knee,' said Father Adams, helpfully on hand as usual.

We explained we were leaving the gap in the window for the swallows but obviously nobody believed it. Fred Ferry, it eventually got back to us through the village grapevine, was putting it down to me getting stuck on that cliff-edge. That was why we didn't put the glass back, he was busily telling people: I was afraid of heights. Not a mere fifteen feet from the ground, I wasn't: I'd have done it without a thought. Charles, who had nerves of steel and could overhang drops of hundreds of feet, would have done it on his head. But it was no good explaining it to the villagers. They all knew better than that.

It was no good, either, trying to explain to Aunt Ethel that we hadn't been in Canada big-game hunting. That was what people had done when she was young. Bear skins, antelope skins, moose heads to hang on the wall... Where were our trophies? she enquired when, on our first Sunday back, Charles fetched her over to lunch. (She'd survived our absence successfully, of course: now she wanted to boast about our exploits.) We hadn't gone for that, we told her. Thinking people didn't kill animals like that nowadays. We'd gone to see and enjoy the living animals. Those were all we'd brought back...

We indicated a pair of cattle horns that hung over the living-room archway, beneath the dark oak beams. They were Texas Long-horns, from a steer that had been bred for beef, and we'd bought them already mounted. They had a span of almost a yard and were really very impressive. Charles had chosen them himself and carried them on to the plane, a sock bound protectively round each tip. He couldn't wrap the rest of them – they were far too big – and they had created quite a sensation. His tooth on the way out, a pair of horns on the way home... Charles always added variety to our travels.

'They're Texas Longhorns,' we shouted at Aunt Ethel now: her hearing aid wasn't working properly as usual. 'From a *steer*. You know – *cattle*, bred for beef. We bought them in Montana.' Aunt Ethel regarded them with approval. She obviously hadn't heard a word we'd said. 'Whichever of you got those,' she said with pride, 'must have been a very good shot.'

So, back in our old routine, we moved on towards Christmas. Charles busy with his orchard, I riding, writing, doing the house-work, taking the cats for walks in the woods in the afternoons.

We didn't give them the freedom Solomon and Sheba had had. There were more people around now with dogs. More strangers, too, who drove out from town to go for walks and might have fancied a Siamese out on the loose. So we let them out for a run before breakfast, started calling them if they weren't back in half an hour... Shebalu was usually back well within that time, but Seeley sometimes went further afield. Up the Forestry lane, perhaps, looking for mice in the ruins, or going up through our woods to Mrs Pursey's where he would sit hopefully by the birdtable in her bungalow garden, visible to every bird for miles.

Mrs Pursey would ring us if she saw him. She knew we didn't like him being even that far away. She was always afraid, she said, that he might go further, and someone who didn't know he was ours might pick him up... And I would trudge off up the hill to fetch him, carrying him back down to the cottage on my shoulder, hoping nobody would see me and feeling a fool for making such a fuss. The neighbours' cats stayed out day and night without harm – but they, I told myself, weren't Siamese. Valuable, attractive, and – discounting all that – with a genius for getting themselves into trouble.

On odd occasions he would be away for an hour or more, and, having checked that he wasn't at Mrs Pursey's, I would go charging round the lanes shrieking 'Seeley-weeley-weeley' and banging a spoon on his feeding plate. As I flashed past, neighbours would ask if it was the big dark one again, and say they'd let me know if they saw him. I've no doubt they tapped their heads at each other when I'd gone. I would have done the same. But I knew Siamese. I never had any peace until – by which time I was usually on my knees – I'd report back to the cottage for the umpteenth time and Charles, keeping watch at base, would call 'He's back' – and sure enough, as large as life, there he'd be sitting in the path. Where on earth had I Been? his air of puzzlement would enquire. He'd been waiting here for me for Ages. What on earth possessed me to run about shouting like that? Didn't I realise he wanted his breakfast?

He didn't play truant very often, but it was always the same when he did. I'd be frantic in case he was in trouble – even while, tearing from one to another of his haunts, I was telling myself not to be so stupid. 'You know he always comes back,' I'd think. As had Solomon, our other wanderer, before him. The number of times I'd rushed around the lanes thinking that Solomon had gone for good...

Once they came in for breakfast, they stayed in for the rest of the day. There were adders on the hills in summer – Seeley, as a kitten, had been bitten up in Annabel's field. Strangers around, people with dogs, adders – for their own safety we kept them in. Until in the late afternoon, working at my typewriter, I'd realised that a deputation had arrived. From their window-seat in the sun, or their armchair, if it was winter, and they were sitting watching me, side by side. Time to go out now, they would inform me. Before Charles started asking about tea.

Invariably I went with them, carrying a golf club for their protection. I didn't take them as far as Solomon and Sheba used to go. Dogs seemed to appear these days from nowhere and the cats were vulnerable on the open track. I either sat with them on the hillside behind the cottage or took them into the woods.

At first just into the pine wood, where they followed me like dogs; Shebalu close behind me, in my footsteps like Wenceslas's page; Seeley loitering at a distance to show his independence, but never letting me out of his sight. If I sat down, Shebalu was on my knees in an instant; she didn't like the feel of the pine needles under her feet. When I looked round, sure enough Seeley would be sitting too... upright, a few feet distant... conveying the impression that he was a Big Cat and nothing to do with us, but following us as soon as we moved on.

Some two hundred yards up the Forestry track there is a beech wood and after a while I began to take them into that. It was lighter – in winter, such sun as there was struck warm in the shelter of the trees and the cats loved chasing each other through the leaves. Up trees, down trees, charging around like pint-sized elephants; pretending they couldn't hear me calling them, then catching me up at a tremendous lick; then back to the cottage in procession, for an evening in front of the fire. I would think how much the woods were like those in Canada. All it needed was a bear or two, or a moose. But then it wouldn't be safe for the cats to be around in. Here, I told myself so many times... here they were so safe.

That Christmas, having resisted it for years, we installed television at the cottage. When we were going to find time to watch it was a problem, of course. We had so many other things to do. We liked having friends in for a natter round the fire for instance, and we liked reading: Charles did his painting in the evenings and it was the only time I had to play the piano. But we ought to have it for the news and the nature programmes, we decided – and, after our trip, I fancied seeing an occasional cowboy film, with cattle milling over the rangeland, riders racing in a cloud of dust out from a ranch... and, in nostalgic imagination, Charles and I riding with them on Sheba and Biz.

So we had it installed, switched it on – I remember the first time was when we were having tea by the fire with the long, low coffee table between us, and both cats were sitting on Charles's lap. I was moving about with crumpets and teacups between Charles and the television set – but it was Seeley who objected to the interruption to his viewing, not Charles. Claws clamped to Charles's knees, eyes concentrated as blue binoculars, he dodged his head impatiently round me when I got between him and the screen. Nearly missed that bit, said his expression. What was the man on that horse doing now? Why on earth couldn't I sit Down!

It reminded me of someone I knew who once bred a litter of television-addicted kittens. She said it was the only thing that kept those seal-point beatniks quiet. They used to come rushing in when the set was switched on and sit in a gang in front of it. They liked cow-boy films the best, she said, and when I asked her how she knew, she told me they never fought or budged an inch while those were on. They were always a bloodthirsty lot, she admitted. She thought they liked hearing the guns go bang.

Aunt Ethel liked cowboy films, too. It was a great help when she came to stay with us and we could park her and Seeley in front of the set. (Shebalu, completely uninterested, always curled in a ball behind Seeley and slept.) We left them like that one night when we had to make a call in the village. They were watching a film about Mexican bandits and there were even more horses than usual charging round, and people escaping across the Rio Grande, and gunfights and a band of hostile Apaches.

Tim Bannett called while we were out and wondered what on earth was going on. Aunt Ethel had the set turned up, of course, being rather deaf. Tim said it sounded from the front gate as if we were having a private revolution – and when he came up the path and knocked at the door he got no answer. Only a burst of gunfire and, when he tapped on the window, a voice yelling 'Take that, you lousy cur!'

He went back home and telephoned us twice, but couldn't get any reply. Somewhat alarmed – wondering whether something had happened to us – he came down to the cottage again. He hammered on the door and window. Still there was no reply. He was very relieved when he rang us later that night and we answered. Fancy, he said, people like us becoming television addicts... He was glad he and Liz didn't have a set. I'm still not sure whether he believed us when we said it was Aunt Ethel and Seeley.

Round about then we heard of a piece of real-life adventure. A Canadian Government official in London, writing to acknowledge our thanks for making possible our trip, said he thought we'd like to know he'd been out in Alberta recently and had actually seen two of the Jasper wolves while driving through the Park. It was winter, the Park was under snow and practically deserted; a very different place from the way it looked in summer. The wolves had come down to look for food and he'd spotted them by the roadside. He'd driven past very slowly and they'd come out and trotted after him. He'd slowed the car even more, driving for several miles at a crawl with the wolves following only yards behind. Then, having an appointment in Banff, he'd had to speed up and they'd turned off into the forest. He'd never seen wolves as close as that before, he concluded. Didn't we think it was interesting?

We did. Knowing something now about them we also had an idea as to why they'd done it. The car going slowly... not at the usual speed of motor traffic. Dropping to a crawl... becoming, to all intents and purposes, even more feeble... no doubt the wolves were following it waiting for it to come to a stop and die. When, though all the evidence says they wouldn't have touched the driver, presumably they were anticipating to be able to eat the car!

Before we knew it, it was March and the primroses were out along the banks of the stream. Then it was May, and to Charles's joy the swallows came back again. One morning, as if by magic, there were three tired swallows sitting on the telephone wire. Presumably the original pair and one of their offspring, whom we hoped would also take up quarters in the garage. The third one disappeared later that day, however – probably up to the farm, where there'd be a selection of mates to choose from – and our pair settled down to live with us again. There was no cautiousness now as to whether we were a safe proposition. They remembered us and set to repairing their nest at once. We watched the male bird for ages, bringing hay from Annabel's stable... flying over with a long strand in its beak, circling several times to get it horizontal, then, with the hay out behind it like a kite-tail, straight in through the window gap at full speed.

Now it was June. Tim still hadn't got his goat but he was very busy with his bees. Putting on supers, removing queen cells to prevent the hive from swarming – he'd become very competent indeed and it wasn't his bees that were seen one morning clustered on one of the chimneys at he farm, looking as if they d been glued to it with treacle and showing every sign of settling in. Nobly, however, he and a neighbour tried to get them down – and were well and truly stung for their pains. Up on a roof, on a ladder, is not the best place to argue with bees. Gorged with honey, as they are when they swarm, they wouldn't in the normal way have been angry, but this lot appeared to have mislaid their queen and were very agitated indeed. Just as Tim's neighbour, Henry, got near them with a box, they swept up and off again.

Circling, they came down on the next-door-but-one chimney, presumably thinking the queen might be there – seeing which, the owner of the cottage, who'd been watching from the garden, rushed in and lit a fire with the intention of smoking them off. What he'd forgotten was that he'd blocked the chimney for the summer, to stop stray birds and soot from falling down, and in next to no time the scene was one of animation such as is rarely seen in our village. A ladder on the farm roof, another against the cottage wall, Tim and Henry comparing bee-stings in the lane, smoke pouring spectacularly out of the cottage windows and Miss Wellington wanting to phone the fire brigade. The postman stopped to watch, a string of riders joined the throng, everybody gawking at the swarm on the chimney top – where they remained for quite a while until, still unsettled, they took off again. Definitely they weren't Tim Bannett's bees. Equally definitely, he got the blame.

Then it was July. A whole year had gone by since our trip to Alberta and we recalled it nostalgically day by day. This time last year it had been Klondike Days. This time last year, we were at Wapiti. Then came the anniversary of the day we went on the wolf-howl the day that had been so wonderful. This year it was one of the most tragic we had ever known. It was the day we lost Seeley.

# Thirteen

THE PREVIOUS DAY HAD been such a pleasant one. We had gone down to the moors in the afternoon, to buy peat for the garden. We took tea with us and had it in the car, looking out at the rhines and the flat water meadows and the hedges of pollarded willows that make this corner of Somerset so reminiscent of the Camargue. We watched the herons flying home, and a water-rat sitting up in a clump of reeds eating a seed-head, turning it in his paws as if it were corn-on-the-cob. We came home and I took the cats for a run... then in for their supper and ours. We ate in armchairs so that we could see *The Pallisers*... Shebalu turning her back on such mundane behaviour as usual, Seeley watching eagerly with us. He sat on Charles's knee, that being his favourite viewing point, which gave him an unobscured view of the screen. I looked across at him once. He was looking at me. He squeezed his eyes affectionately, which was always his way of communicating. Later, I remember, he was rolling happily on the carpet and I got down and hugged him, always a pushover for that little black pansy face. Really, I said, when we went to bed... I'd really enjoyed that day.

We let them out next morning, which was Sunday, and they ambled as usual up to the vegetable garden to eat grass and see what the day was like. Charles went with them, to check there were no cars about, and to open the greenhouse door and water the tomatoes. While I was setting breakfast I looked out through the kitchen and Seeley had come back and was sitting in the outer doorway. He was looking out into the yard, obviously wondering where to go next. I almost fetched him in – but he hadn't been out long, I thought. It was such a nice morning. Another ten minutes or so wouldn't hurt. So I left him. Shebalu came back while we were having breakfast. But we never saw Seeley again.

It was Charles who became anxious first. Out in the garden watching for him after breakfast, he'd noticed a girl with a limping wolfhound come up the lane. Always suspicious since Seeley had been chased up a tree down there – why was the dog limping? he wondered. After that a gang of boys came past, pulling at branches and kicking stones. We'd better start to look for him, said Charles. There were too many people about.

I went up to Mrs Pursey's. She hadn't seen him at all. I came back and went, calling him persistently, up the Forestry Lane. Not right to the top. His range didn't normally extend that far and I was wasting time, I thought. If he *was* up there, he was safer than on the road. Better to concentrate on the hill.

Back to the cottage, up the hill once more – this time right to the Rose and Crown, and on up the next hill and along the lane that runs along the top of our woods and then dips to the valley again. I was passing the little paddock where, years before, I'd rescued Solomon by the scruff of his neck from an angry goose, when across in the Forest there was a fusillade of shots and my heart sank like a stone.

Rubbish, I told myself. People wouldn't fire that many shots at a cat. Besides, the shots were well over in the Forest. Or were they? Could they perhaps have been at the top of the Forestry lane, or in the beech wood? Sounds echo so much around here. It was too much of a coincidence, though, for Seeley to be missing for two hours and *then* run into a gang with guns. He'd be back by the time I got home.

He wasn't. Charles, returning from searching the other tracks he might have taken, said there was no sign of him on any of them. All the same, we searched them again. We called and hunted all day and the door stayed open all night. We went to bed at midnight from sheer exhaustion but at three in the morning, unable to sleep, I came down, went out into the garden and called again. I came down every night for a week, always hoping that this time he'd be there. One of my most desolate memories is of the yard door open, the darkness outside and the night wind blowing, and my going outside and calling and calling... always without reply. The coldness permeated the living room where he and Shebalu had slept for so long. Their armchair was empty now. Shebalu slept with us upstairs. We searched, and theorised – the whole village searched with us for weeks. But we never found any trace.

Could a fox have taken him? Hardly at nine o'clock on a summer's morning, with Seeley having in the past stood up to big dogs and so many climbable trees around. In any case he would have put up a fight if he'd been attacked and, watching out for him as we'd done, we would have heard it. Could he have been bitten by an adder? There are lots of them round here. Seeley had been bitten as a kitten. He'd screamed so loudly then, though, that the whole valley had heard him, and we would have heard him this time. In any case, said a Vet whom I asked, he wouldn't have collapsed on the spot. He'd have managed to get home.

All the same we checked the countryside all round the valley. We found no body. No trace of blood. No sign of cartridge cases in the Forestry lane. Neither were there any traps around; we searched every hedgerow for those. We combed the undergrowth on either side all the way up the hill in case he'd been hit by a car and had crawled away, though, so far as we know, no car had been around. The road ends in front of the cottage; after that it is a bridle track. Few strange cars come down here, and even then not fast – the hill is too steep and winding for that. We searched all the same, just in case. But there wasn't a single sign.

Had there been a car parked at the top of the hill where we couldn't see it, the occupants perhaps having gone for a walk, and Seeley, always a great one for poking around cars, had got into it and been carried off? Maybe, if that had happened, the people had turned him out when they found him, which could have been miles away. Maybe on the other hand, they were looking after him, not knowing where he'd got in. In case that had happened, and because he was so well known, after he'd been missing for almost a week, an appeal was put out in the newspapers and on radio and television, asking if anyone had seen him.

We got the first phone call, from a farmer forty miles away, within minutes of the television broadcast. There had been a large stray Siamese in one of his fields for the past five days, he said – catching the rabbits and sleeping in his haybarn. It was right by the side of the Castle Cary road where a passing car might have dumped him. Beside ourselves with joy – it *must* be Seeley, we thought; absolutely the right number of days that he'd been missing: and how many other big, dark-backed Siamese could there be astray in this pan of Somerset? – we drove down with his basket to fetch him. The farmer took us to the field and I called, but it was dark by this time and no cat came. After an hour we drove home – still sure it must be him – and were back again at first light next morning. It was lost, right enough. And it was a seal-point Siamese. But it wasn't Seeley.

We concealed our heartbreak. How strange, we said, that there should be another stray Siamese as well. The farmer said we needn't worry, it wouldn't be stray for long. If its owner didn't turn up he'd take it on himself. 'Very intelligent, that cat is,' he said. He was telling us! In its adversity it had found a haybarn to sleep in, rabbits for the eating, a stream to drink from nearby... and, if it so wanted, another home where it would be welcome, with a prosperous farmer under its thumb. We hoped that Seeley, if he was alive, had been equally fortunate. We hoped, even more, that we would find him. Then we drove back to the cottage where a friend, keeping vigil by the phone, reported that another call had come in.

Siamese cats get lost all right. In the next few weeks we followed up more calls than we would ever have believed possible from people who had seen cats in their gardens whom they were positive must be Seeley. We went to see every one. Nine times out of ten it transpired that the cat lived across the road, round the corner, or in some cases wasn't a Siamese at all. We did, however, see six seal-point neuters in three weeks, all in the West of England, that were completely and hopelessly lost, obviously miles from their homes, with no clue as to how they had got there.

The thing that upset us every time, apart from the fact that it was never Seeley, was the fear and bewildered hopelessness that looked at us out of those lost blue eyes. Cats that had been so cherished, forced to fend for themselves. If we could, we'd have given a home to all of them, but we couldn't take on six... and obviously somebody somewhere, like us, was grieving and searching for them. Their best chance of being found was to leave them where they were. In each case the person who had contacted us was quietly keeping an eye on them. The only thing we ourselves could do was to go on hoping and asking and searching.

Our worst experience was when a farmer's wife rang us one night from five miles away, to say she'd seen a Siamese cat hunting round their barn at dusk for several evenings and she wondered whether we'd found ours yet. No we hadn't we said. We'd come over at once... Oh, it wasn't there now, she said. She was just checking to see if we'd found Seeley. She'd watch out, and if the cat appeared again, she'd ring us as soon as she saw it.

For two nights we heard nothing, so I rang her to enquire. No, she hadn't seen it again, she said. Then on the third night, she rang us to say her husband had found it. It had been hit by a car and was dead. It was ten o'clock, and dark, but we drove over at once. I couldn't rest without knowing but when we got there, I couldn't look at the body. Charles had to do it. And, by dim torchlight in a shed, he thought at first it was Seeley.

'If only we'd come over the night she rang us, and I'd called him,' I said. There are so many 'if only's'. If only I had brought Seeley in from the doorstep that morning... And we had called so much, so futilely, in so many different places. Then I looked at the dead cat, forcing myself to do it. If it was Seeley, I had to wish him goodbye. And hope surged through my heart again, because I knew it *wasn't* Seeley. 'It's not his face,' I said. We lifted the cat out of the box and shone the torch more closely on it, and sure enough, its back, too, was too light. I wept for the dead cat, and for the owner who had lost him – and gave thanks that it wasn't Seeley.

It might as well have been. At least we would have known his end. As it is, we never shall. So many people told us of missing Siamese that had been found as much as a whole year later. The one that walked home from Wales to Sussex, for instance, taking a year to do it. And the one that vanished from its home one day and the owners hunted and advertised futilely... until six months later there was a phone call from a farmer who lived a few miles away. He'd just heard they'd lost a Siamese, he said. There'd been one living wild in his wood all the winter. They went over and called and their cat emerged from the trees, glad to see them and fit as a trivet. The only difference in him was the tremendous depth of his coat, which had automatically thickened for his protection.

So many tales we heard to give us hope, but it is over a year now since we lost him. Sometimes we wonder whether he is still alive – and at other times know that he can't be. If he was killed, we hope it was quick and he knew nothing about it. If someone has him, we hope that they love him as much as we did. It is the worst way to lose a friend... not to know the end, and always to be wondering.

It would never happen again, said Charles. Any cats we had would never again be out of our sight. To which end we bought a collar for Shebalu and fitted a twenty-foot nylon lead to it. Charles took her into the orchard on it in the mornings, and it was surprising how quickly she got used to it. She seemed to think it was some special bond – a sort of token of her and Charles's togetherness. She purred when it was put on, learned not to pull on it, undoubtedly felt it akin to a Lady Mayoress's collar... which didn't alter the fact that at the first opportunity she took off in it, lead and all.

She had been up in the vegetable garden eating grass and Charles had left her for just a moment to open the greenhouse. No more than a *second*, he panted, racing down to the kitchen to fetch me, and when he turned round she had gone. It was only a fortnight since we'd lost Seeley. Supposing there was a rogue fox around... or a killer dog, or someone who didn't like Siamese cats, and now Shebalu in her turn met up with them? Worst of all, she was trailing a 20-foot nylon cord which could get tangled up in anything. Our minds rocketing from one possibility to another, we tore around like agitated ants.

Fortunately I found her within minutes, having picked the right direction by sheer chance. She must have gone straight up the ten-foot wall at the back of the garden, which was how she'd vanished so quickly, and she was up in Annabel's field, hiding in a clump of bracken, thoroughly enjoying the search. Her lead rustled in the bracken as she turned her head to watch me and I heard it as I went past. When I stooped to look, there she was, eyes crossed with self-satisfaction. Nearly missed her, hadn't I? she said.

After that there was no letting go of her lead in the mornings. Whoever was with her stayed firmly on the end of it. Only in the afternoons did she ever run free, when she came up with me on the hillside. Now, though, I didn't sit on a rug as I used to do, waiting for her and Seeley to come back from their undergrowth-inspecting sorties. When Shebalu went round a corner I was right behind her. She was never out of my sight. We walked in the woods together. We sat under the oak tree in Annabel's field – Shebalu perched on my knee, surveying the valley below. She would watch the track through the bracken... waiting, it was obvious, for Seeley to come along it; wondering where on earth he could be.

One afternoon in September, walking with her through Annabel's field, for once I was in the lead. She'd stopped to sniff the moss under a wayfaring bush and I'd gone around it and on along the path. Suddenly realising she wasn't with me, I went back in a panic. Something I wouldn't have done in the old days, knowing she'd be bounding after me at any moment, but now I couldn't take a chance.

It was just as well I did go back because when I rounded the bush Shebalu was experimentally patting at an adder. A young one, rather sleepy – she must have scented it and scooped it out of the undergrowth – but an adder, potentially lethal, all the same. I remember looking at it disbelievingly, thinking 'Not this, as well as Seeley' – and in an instant I had grabbed Shebalu, thrown her away to safety down the hillside, and hit the adder with the golf-club I always carried when out with the cats. I killed it, hating the necessity, but there was nothing else to be done. It obviously had a hole under the under-growth and, had I left it, Shebalu would have searched it out again. Followed by her, I carried it back to the cottage draped over the golf-club and called Charles to look at it. He confirmed that it was an adder. We might have lost Shebalu. Honestly, we wondered, what on earth was going on?

We guarded her even more carefully after that. Being Shebalu, she enjoyed it. She slept with us at night. She followed me like a shadow during the day – upstairs, downstairs, perched importantly on the kitchen table or the bathroom stool, her small blue face jutting urgently as she nattered at me non-stop. Did she like being the only one? More probably, we decided, she was lonely, and in the absence of Seeley was attaching herself more closely to us. Certainly, even after weeks had passed, there were still times when she sat watching expectantly out of the window – or, when she was eating, looked round as if another cat should be there.

For ourselves, we missed Seeley as much as ever – stretched out luxuriously on the hearthrug; yelling for the hall door to be opened... he never learned to open it for himself. Bounding down the stairs ahead of us, his back legs spread wide in exuberance. A dark head, as well as a blue one, thrust enquiringly into the refrigerator. We still hoped we would find him – but now it was November. Four months since he'd vanished, and the hurt hadn't grown any less. For our sake, as well as Shebalu's, we decided to get another kitten... and hope that, Siamese being so contrary, that might bring Seeley back.

# Fourteen

WHEN SOLOMON DIED WE were determined to find a successor who'd grow up to look as like him as possible. Armed with his pedigree, and photographs of him as a kitten, it had taken us a month to find Seeley. Now, in turn, we wanted a kitten who'd look like him – and we wanted one as soon as possible. We'd been without a seal-point boy for four months now, and it was already far too long.

We rang Seeley's breeder. She had met tragedy, too. Seeley's father was dead. Not, as we'd always privately feared would be his end, from his habit of wandering off on romantic expeditions – he having been an exception, a pedigree stud-cat who was always allowed his freedom. It happened because the people next door had bought some guinea pigs for their children, and thoughtlessly put down poison for the rats who came after the guinea pigs' food and Orlando, spending a few quiet days at home for once, had brought in one of the poisoned rats and eaten it. Nine years without a mishap and he'd had to die like that, said his owner. If only she'd called the Vet as soon as he was sick. But she'd thought at first it was just a stomach upset, and by the time she found the half-eaten rat it was too late.

Orlando was gone. Seeley's mother had died, too. There was no possibility of getting a closely related kitten. Wondering where to try next, we remembered a cat we had gone to see when we were looking for Seeley. Someone had phoned us to say he was sitting, looking lost, in a field about two miles away from the cottage. We'd rushed over at once – and indeed it did appear to be Seeley, sitting on a plank in a field behind some houses, apparently watching for mice. If Seeley had gone down through the Valley this was where he would have come out and it was just the owlish way he adopted when he was watching things. Perhaps he'd been hunting in the woods on the way, we thought, and it had taken him several days to get there.

We were sure it was him this time. Charles waited with his basket at the edge of the field while I approached slowly through the long grass so as not to frighten him. I held out my hand and called his name. He turned his face towards me and sat waiting. The size, the big dark back, the expression on his face... my heart rose at every step. Only when I reached him did I know that, again, it wasn't Seeley. When Charles and I came back out of the field a man who'd been passing and had stopped to watch us said he thought the cat belonged to people who'd just come to live up on the hill. If we could find out who they were and where they'd got him, it now occurred to us, we might still be able to get a kitten who looked like Seeley.

We managed to trace him. He'd come from a breeder near Bridgwater and of all the extraordinary coincidences, not only was he distantly related to Seeley, but he and Shebalu had the same father. Shebalu's mother, a blue-point like her, had been mated to a lilac-point called Valentine. A famous Champion of Champions, he was, owned by a Mrs Furber. We'd never actually seen Valentine, though, and it seemed almost as if it was meant that he should be the father of the cat in the field... and, when we enquired, that Mrs Furber also owned the seal-point mother.

We rang her. She said she had two litters of kittens almost ready but neither of them, unfortunately, was directly Valentine's. One litter was his daughter's, though, and his descendants invariably came out like him: we'd be practically certain of getting one from that lot who would look like the cat in the field. On the other hand there was a kitten in the elder litter, sired by Saturn, who was really quite exceptional. She'd never had a kitten quite like him. Lively, intelligent – you could see him sizing you up when he looked at you, she said. He stood out from the others like a sore thumb.

He stood out for another reason, too. Inquisitive and enterprising, at three weeks old he'd got his tail caught in a door. It now had a bend in it – at the base end, not a Siamese kink – which spoilt him from being the show cat he otherwise would have been. Apart from this he was absolutely gorgeous and as she knew we liked cats of character... honestly, she said, she couldn't have picked a better match. He was absolutely made for us.

Sorry, I told her. Our cats had all been perfect. It would seem all wrong to have one with a bend in its tail. Besides, we'd set our heart on a kitten of Valentine's... if there wasn't one of his available we'd rather have one of his daughter's. All right, she said. If we liked to come and choose one, it would be ready in a fortnight.

We went the following Saturday. We didn't take a basket. After all, we were only going down to see them. We walked into the Furbers' sitting-room without so much as a thought about the kitten who'd bent his tail... and guess who we brought home with us?

When we went in. Valentine's daughter's kittens were tumbling around the room like particularly exuberant clowns in a circus. Kittens in the coal-scuttle, kittens whizzing over the chairs and up the curtains... we'd seen it so often before. There is nothing in this world more captivating than a litter of Siamese kittens and I was among them, on my knees, in an instant... only to see, in front of me on the hearthrug, a perspex travelling box with two larger kittens in it. One had a bent tail and was looking indignant; the other had a firmly closed eye. He, said Mrs Furber, indicating the one who resembled Nelson, was one she'd thought we might possibly like to see... in case we wanted to take one away with us, instead of waiting for the younger litter. 'Believe me,' she said, 'he was *perfect* when I fetched him in. I brought the one with the bent tail just to keep him company. I ought to have known better, of course. He'd poked him in the eye.'

It seemed that the one with the bent tail excelled at getting the others into trouble. He was always the one, said Mrs Furber, who led the way up on to ledges in their run that were just about the cat equivalent of climbing Everest – and then, when the others had got themselves all hopelessly stuck, he'd jump down and leave them stranded. She'd seen him do it so often and whenever she went to the rescue there, invariably, he'd be: the little, round-eyed innocent, regarding them puzzledly from the ground. One day, she said, he'd managed to move the prop that held the cat-house window open: something no other cat or kitten had ever done. *He'd* got through before the window came down. The others, following after him, had nearly been port-cullised.

She'd better let him out now, she said, looking at the travelling box. She'd put the two of them in there to keep them apart from the younger litter. But he was getting rather restless. He'd be hitting his brother in the other eye at any moment.

She opened the travelling box door and he came out like a small, charging bull. Up on to the settee, where he rolled, waving his paws and arching his back in celebration. Then, hearing me laugh, he got up and galloped to the edge to stare at me. His eyes were almost hypnotic. They bore deeply into mine, as though he was either reading my thoughts or trying to imprint me with some of his. He stood there for several seconds before he lowered his head and charged away, launching himself off the settee to land like a bomb in the middle of the younger kittens who, with frantic squeals for Mum, shot for shelter in all directions. They had been playing with a marble, which Bent Tail now took over. 'He likes marbles. They're noisier than ping-pong balls,' Mrs Furber explained as he dribbled it like lightning round the room. 'Whatever he's doing he shows off, wanting to get people's attention.'

He had ours, all right. He aimed the marble expertly under the settee and flushed out three of Valentine's grandchildren. The entire entourage disappeared under a nearby chair and we could see odd paws waving wildly about. The marble rolled out... was hooked back again... there was what sounded like a rugby scrum. Whoever came out behind the marble, I announced eventually, was the kitten we would have. I was cheating, of course. I knew who'd come out. He emerged behind the marble, bent tail triumphant. I picked him up. Again I got that solemn, hypnotic stare. 'Welcome to the family,' I said.

Accompanying the solemn stare was a solemn little seal-point nose that reminded us of the saskatoon berries we'd seen in Canada. That was why we named him Saskatoon Seal, which has since become Saska, or Sass. Then Mrs Furber took us out to see his father, whom she said he was very like. On the way we saw Valentine, Shebalu's father, who was sitting regally in his run. A beautiful, elegant lilac-point – we could see where his daughter got her looks from. He rubbed his head on the run-wire when Mrs Furber spoke to him. He had a wonderful nature, she said. She could go into his run and handle him even when he had a queen with him for mating.

Saturn now, she said – leading us over to another run from which a big seal-point male was regarding us with undisguised suspicion – when *he* had a queen in there with him he treated the place like an Eastern seraglio. Flew at the wire when anyone as much as passed, in case they were trying to steal her. He was as lovable as anything at other times – but a real Tarzan character, not a bit like Valentine. 'Look at their runs,' she said. 'Valentine's is always so neat and tidy – I never mind anyone seeing it. But Saturn absolutely refuses to use an earthbox and he *will* spray over his house.'

Valentine's run indeed looked as if it ought to be in *Ideal Homes* and the paint-work on his house was immaculate. Saturn's run appeared to have been dug to plant potatoes; and the paint, where he persistently sprayed on it, was yellowed and peeling in strips. It was as if he'd put up a notice 'This is My House- Keep Off', and we laughed. He certainly was a character we said. We hoped Saska would take after him. A remark I remembered next morning when we found that Sass, too, had a quirk about earthboxes.

To be fair, it might have been traumatic. We'd arranged to take him home with us in the evening – we had to go on to Watchet and we called for him on our way back. It was dark by then and, as we hadn't a basket, I tucked him inside my coat. He was warm, but we were strangers and he was frightened. He spat at us all the way back. None of the others had ever done that: I hoped he was going to be good-tempered, I said. It was the darkness, Charles assured me. He was scared because he couldn't see us, and of the noise of the engine, and of the lights of the other cars going past. It showed what a plucky little chap he was – so frightened, but he wouldn't give in.

He was scared all right. When we got home I put him in our big, wire-fronted cat-basket. He'd feel more secure in there, I said. then we let Shebalu in to meet him. We thought she'd be a little wary at first. When we first brought her home as a kitten, Seeley had been terrified of her for days. What we weren't prepared for was Shebalu marching up to the basket, glaring in at him with her face to the cage-front and giving a tremendous, explosive spit. I jumped yards at the vehemence of it and I wasn't even on the receiving end. Sass jumped as high as he could in the confines of the basket and had diarrhoea on the spot.

Shebalu slept with us as usual that night, while Sass stayed down by the fire. I'd cleaned out the basket, put a blanket and hotwater bottle in it, and another blanket on the hearthrug in front of the fire. I left the basket door open: he could sleep inside it if he felt safer, or out on the second blanket, nearer the fire, if he preferred. It would be his own small retreat till Shebalu and he got together.

I thought that, like his father, he would feel more secure with a lair of his own.

We gave him his supper, put down water and an earthbox for him and, collecting Shebalu from the kitchen where she was shouting her head off from the top of the cooker with a spit from him as we passed the basket, we went hopefully to bed. It was always the same, we told ourselves. There were always these ructions at first. But Shebalu was young, and a female – she'd soon get round to mothering him. It wasn't the same as having Seeley back, but it was good to have two cats again.

Even when we came down next morning and discovered that his earthbox was dry as the Sahara but the blanket in front of his basket was wet, I wasn't particularly perturbed. When our first Siamese, Sugieh, had had kittens, they had done that at first – wetted the old dressing gown I'd wrapped round their basket as a draught-excluder until Sugieh trained them to a box. Sass, Charles and I decided, had just been following his primeval instinct. What with being parted from his Mum, and Shebalu frightening him, and finding himself suddenly alone in a strange place, he'd nipped out from the basket, used the blanket as the nearest thing... probably in his mind he was staking out his terrain... He'd be perfectly all right now it was daylight and he could see it was safe to use his box.

To which end, as Shebalu was slinking sinisterly round the room crossing her eyes at him from behind chairs, I gave him his breakfast in our bedroom, showed him his earthbox filled with peat in the corner, and put him and a freshly-filled hotwater bottle in a nest of sweaters on the bed. A time-honoured refuge, this: it had been a favourite with all our cats. I left him curled in it blissfully; such a self-contained little white ball. Later, I brought him down so that he could be with Charles and let Shebalu go upstairs. If she could sniff at her leisure round the place where he'd been sleeping, I thought, she'd soon get used to the smell of him. But why was she regarding the sweaters with such horror and trying to rake them over with her paw? Because, I discovered when I touched them, he'd wetted on those as well.

We spent the rest of the day putting him in and out of earthboxes. At one point we had six in a row containing, in that order, peat moss, ordinary peat, earth, sawdust and torn-up paper – and then, just for luck, earth again. They stretched in a line through the kitchen, past the refrigerator. I put him in each one in turn. He hesitated in the sawdust as if it rang some faint small bell in his memory, then marched nonchalantly on down the line. Eventually I rang Mrs Furber, who was absolutely mortified. He was a little horror, she said. He *did* know about earthboxes. Like the others, he'd been trained to use one. She'd watched him sit on it again and again. It was just like him to let her down. He was obviously doing it deliberately. Did we want to bring him back?

Never, I said – but what did she use in her earthboxes? Sawdust, she told me: or failing that, torn-up newspapers. I remembered his hesitation at the sawdust... it had meant something, but maybe that had been damp. Charles, ever valiant, went out and sawed some logs to get some more. Hearing the noise of sawing outside in the yard on a dark Sunday night... Boy, we were back to normal! I thought.

I presented the sawdust to Sass. What was that for? he demanded. We played musical chairs with him down the line of boxes again. This time, to our joy, he did do a small puddle in the peat-box and we went to bed congratulating ourselves that we'd won. He had a fresh blanket to sleep on – in the armchair this time – and, which he obviously liked very much, a hotwater bottle tucked inside it, and a cushion to keep out the draughts. In front of the chair, where he couldn't possibly miss it, we put an earthbox filled with peat. When we came down next morning, he'd wetted the blanket again.

# Fifteen

LOOKING BACK, WE CAN only conclude that he did it because he was so intelligent. According to his lights – you could tell it by the earnestness on his face – he was being the cleanest of kittens. He'd come to a strange house where the first thing that had happened was that a big cat had frightened him into using a blanket as an earthbox. Ergo, if it was woollen things... blankets and sweaters and such... that people used as earthboxes in this house... who was *he* to argue? Blankets and sweaters he'd use.

That, at any rate, is the only explanation we could find for the fact that during the weeks that followed we'd get him for maybe as much as a day or two to use a box of peat or sawdust... looking terribly worried while he did so but if we *insisted*, said his expression... then, presumably scared at what his guardian angel would think of such a relapse, back he'd go to the smell of wool again. We had to harden our hearts and make him sleep without a blanket. He looked so small and forlorn, curled in the armchair on a cotton cushion. We even had to wrap his bottle in a towel. Wrap it in wool and he'd wet it – and then, to show how clean he really was, drag the whole thing out of the chair and dump it in the middle of the hearthrug. Couldn't sleep with that smell, he said. Lavatories belonged on the Floor.

By making him sleep on cotton for a while we cured him of wetting wool. When it wasn't available he used his earthbox quite happily. Nowadays he sleeps on a blanket without a second thought. We even trust him with expensive sweaters. For a while, though, obviously to placate that guardian angel, he surreptitiously used the corner of one particular rug in the living-room. We discovered it by seeing him hovering around the spot and looking furtive when he knew we were watching him. After that we put him out in the hall the moment we recognised his rug-using expression – following which, protocol having been decided for him, we would hear him tear up to the spare room to use the Big Cat's box. At night, besides providing him, with about half a hundredweight of peat, we covered that particular rug with a big rubber groundsheet. Putting it down, putting two peat-boxes at one end, weighting the other three sides with a table, the kitchen stool and a horse bronze (otherwise, following the dictates of his conscience, he would pull back the groundsheet to use the rug)... I wouldn't change Sass for anything, I said. But why did it have to happen to us?

Because he was a Siamese, of course, with his own ideas on things, and because, in his first few impressionable moments in his new home, Shebalu had scared him into it. Just as the introduction of a new cat next door to them had led two other Siamese we knew into spraying. Their names were Sugar and Spice and they belonged to Dora and Nita, who were friends of ours, and who also had a Scottie called Dougal. The cats were in residence before Dougal arrived but they graciously condescended to accept him. He in turn adored his girls and considered it his mission in life to defend them – to which end, when this ginger cat started coming into the garden, strolling around as if it owned it, Dougal would dash out, all bark and big feet, and vociferously see it off. This in turn would rouse Sugar and Spice, who'd go out to see what was doing – and, as their contribution to the defence of the realm, obligingly started to spray.

She didn't know girls *could*, Dora said. They could if they were Siamese, I informed her. We'd had a stray cat around the cottage once and our first Sheba had gone round performing like a flit-gun. One day, presumably to mark me among her possessions, she sprayed my gum-boots while I was in them.

They wouldn't have minded so much if Sugar and Spice had confined it to outdoors, said Nita, but they started spraying indoors as well. Over the long velvet curtains – they had plastic bags tacked over those, which they took off when anybody came. Over the sink. On the sitting-room wall – Sugar used spraying for blackmail now; if she wanted to go out and they wouldn't let her, she'd stand on the side-table so they could see her and raise her tail intimidatingly at the wall. She didn't perform immediately. In the first place she'd just stand there and threaten.

We fell about laughing when we heard about the cooker. On a couple of occasions, it seemed, one of the cats (probably Sugar, said Dora: she was the one with the most Machiavellian mind) had stood on the cooker and sprayed the panel which held the control knobs. We could imagine what a time they'd had cleaning those. But the culminating incident had been the time they put the joint in the oven, set the timer and went to church- and when they came back, expecting to be met by the smell of roast beef, they found the oven was still cold. Somebody had sprayed straight into the timer clock and stopped it, and the automatic switch hadn't come on. 'Nobody'd believe it, would they?' asked Nita. Knowing Siamese cats, we would. At least, however, we were able to cure Sass of his fixation in the end. Sugar and Spice still have their moments.

A good deal of Sass's training was carried out by Shebalu. After four days of slinking round like Lucrezia Borgia, looking sinisterly at him round corners, she decided to take him in hand. By this time he'd begun to take on the scent of the place and obviously didn't smell quite so repulsive. He'd also fallen in the fishpond, which had probably helped quite a lot.

Both Solomon and Seeley had fallen in the pond in their time – it seemed to be a tradition with our boys – so I wasn't really surprised when, watching over him while he zoomed round the yard, he chased after a stray late gnat and went into the water with a splash. What did surprise me, rushing to the rescue, was to find there was really no need. Sass, head up, all nine inches of him completely confident, was swimming like a retriever across the pool. I stood there dumbfounded as he climbed out on the other side, his bent tail raised in triumph. *He* wasn't afraid of water, he informed me. They had a big river where *he* was born.

I took him indoors and towelled him down, thus removing even more of his original scent, and that evening, while he was curled on Charles's knee, Shebalu climbed cautiously up beside him. She stretched out her neck, did a tentative lick... from the tiny white bundle came an enthusiastic purr... until Shebalu, progressing, tried to clean the inside of his ears, where the smell of his mother still lurked. 'SCH... AAAH' spat Shebalu. Up went Sass. And Charles started telling me about his nerves.

It wasn't only his nerves that suffered during those early days. Sass, dividing his affection scrupulously between us, decided that I was the one to Love Him – to which end he would follow me round looking for any convenient height (the edge of the bed, for instance, or the bathroom stool) from which he could launch himself at my chest. It was a good thing it was winter and I was wearing hefty sweaters – and there, clinging to me like a koala bear, he would talk to me confidingly while I carried him about.

Charles he delegated as the one to play with him – to which end, besides trailing ties and pieces of string wherever he went around the cottage, Charles was also expected to throw things for him. Sass, as keen a retriever as Shebalu had been as a kitten, would bring back his catnip mouse or his bean-bag with a bell on it over and over again. Charles, trying to read at the same time, would feel for it with one hand and throw it. Sass, watching with impatience the delay which this involved, eventually took to placing the toy on Charles's foot – and, when the groping hand didn't immediately locate it, jumping on it to show where it was and in the process puncturing Charles's ankle. The resultant yells were absolutely blood-curdling.

Charles took to sitting with his trousers rolled up when he was reading, even when Sass didn't appear to be around. It was no good my saying it looked as if he was taking a mustard bath and what would anyone say if they happened to call in. He never knew when the attack would come, he said, and when I said but that wouldn't help his ankles... Maybe not, he said, but at least scratches would heal. That little devil was ruining all his trousers.

So Sass pursued his intrepid way, unmoved by Charles's yelling. He brought his toys for me to throw, too, as a variation from Charles. Then... obviously I didn't come up to scratch on the toy-throwing, either... he started offering them to Shebalu. I looked in from the kitchen one morning when things seemed unnaturally quiet, to see Sass trot across the floor with his bean-bag in his mouth and put it down in front of Shebalu. He sat back hopefully and looked at her. She regarded it for a moment, picked it up in her mouth, shook it gently to rattle the bell, and quite deliberately tossed it. It went only about a foot and she didn't do it again – but it was obvious our blue girl was trying.

How much she loved him was made clear one day when I was giving the living-room a belated clean. She was asleep upstairs on the bed – being so aristocratic she wasn't the least bit interested in housework. Sass, on the other hand, was pottering about with me... turning somersaults on the cushions, continually rushing up my legs. A moment earlier he'd disappeared in pursuit of a pingpong ball and was diving about under the dresser. I finished dusting the mantelshelf, stepped back hard on poor Sass who must have right that moment come zooming back to climb me, and there was a screech as if he'd been flattened.

Immediately there was a thump from upstairs and Shebalu came tearing down to see what had happened. Apologetically I held him out for her to inspect. He was all right, I said. 'Just you be more Careful with him, all the same,' said her look as she licked him proprietorially.

Everybody loved him. Tim Bannett, calling in the morning after his arrival, was so struck by the size of his ears – and by the fact that Sass decided Tim could Love Him too and spent the visit attached like a limpet to his chest – that within minutes of Tim's departure Liz arrived to ask if she could see him. 'Gosh, he's gorgeous,' she said, looking at him admiringly. Sass pointed a pair of ears like big black yacht sails at her. Like him to sit on her sweater too? he asked.

Miss Wellington burst into tears as soon as she saw him, saying he was so like Seeley as a kitten. Father Adams reached out a wistful finger to stroke him. He had once owned a Siamese. It had been our admiration for her, all those years ago, that had led us to getting Sugieh. 'Minds I of Mimi,' he said now. He still pronounced it My-my. 'If I were ten years younger, darned if I 'ouldn't 'ave another.' He needn't worry about that, I told him. Sass was willing to share. I put Sass on Father Adams's waistcoat, where he obligingly did his limpet act. 'How about I then?' Fred Ferry enquired. Sass was transferred to him. Never did I think I'd see sour old Fred stroking a Siamese kitten. ''Ouldn't mind takin' he up to the pub,' he said – and patently there'd have been no objection from Saska. Charles and I had brought him home, however, fully determined on one thing. Neither he nor Shebalu were ever going to be out of our sight – except when we went on holiday and they went to board with the Francises.

Out of doors that was, of course. Indoors it was a different matter. For the sake of our nerves and digestion they had to be shut out in the hall at mealtimes. Which was why, every Siamese worth his salt having his own idea of how to tackle important problems, Sass started trying to chew his way back in via our new mustard carpet.

I could have banged my head on the wall with despair. One has to accept, of course, that Siamese are destructive. Solomon had ripped a hole in the stair-carpet by way of sharpening his claws: he and Sheba, over the years, had demolished two sets of loose covers between them: Seeley's penchant, when he was shut out, had been removing the draught excluders from doors: Shebalu had recently started on a chair. But *carpets*. At the price they are *now*. And not just clawing them but chewing them till they were bare, fringed canvas at the corners... 'What have we let ourselves in for this time?' I wailed, clutching my brow in desperation.

'Another cat who reasons for himself,' said Charles. 'You know you wouldn't want it any other way. In the end you'll think it funny.'

Not as yet I haven't – where, when people come through our front door, the first thing they see is a whacking great vinyl corner piece over the carpet in front of the living-room door. 'It's not to save wear,' I explain when I see them looking at it. 'It's to stop our Siamese chewing the corners.' You can see their eyebrows lift... a *cat* chewing the carpet? I bet they go away and say I'm batty.

There is another vinyl protective piece where the living-room carpet adjoins the kitchen door. Until it was put there, when Sass got tired of waiting for his meals he lay down and chewed on that. There are more frayed edges outside the bathroom and bedroom doors, too, whereby hang a couple of tales. Normally Sass wouldn't bother with the bathroom, there not being anything interesting inside, but one day Shebalu got shut in there by accident, being a great one for hiding behind doors. Sass discovered where she was – we didn't even know she was missing – but did he howl the place down, as our other boys would have done?

No. Sass the Resourceful lay down and tried to chew her out. When I went upstairs, wondering where they were, the corners of *that* carpet had gone.

On the second occasion we'd gone for a walk with friends, shutting the cats out in the hall as usual. They had a hotwater bottle in a nest of sweaters on the bed, an earthbox in the box-room, they could also go into the spare room if they liked and talk to passers-by out of the window... At least, that was the normal arrangement but in the rush of getting ready to go, somebody shut the bedroom door and also the one to the box-room. The only door left open was the one to the spare room, which we use also as a study.

Any of our previous cats would have been perfectly content to be in there – after all, we were only away for an hour – but Sass gets so intense about things, when we got back we found devastation. The carpet in front of the bedroom door was chewed with his trying to get in there. So it was in front of the box-room door because he hadn't been able to get in to his earthbox. Ditto in front of the bathroom door, his second attack on that one: it looked as if a dog had been worrying a slipper.

He'd then gone into the spare room, where there was a car-rug on the settee. You can guess what he did to that. Two puddles, one at either end, to show that This Territory belonged to Sass. *Why* did he have to do that, I asked him? Why couldn't he have held on like other cats? In any case, we'd only been gone an hour – it couldn't have been necessary to go *twice*. Sass looked at me reprovingly. I knew how he worried, he said.

He has been with us for over a year now and we can't imagine the place without him, though we wish – how we wish – there hadn't been such a sad reason for his coming.

He never wets on wool now... that, he assures us, was when he was a Baby. He hasn't given up chewing carpets, though: ours still have vinyl corners. As far as possible we co-operate with him by remembering not to shut doors. Seeley never did learn to push open the hall door from the outside – at five years old he still sat outside and bawled for admission, or waited for Shebalu to open it when he would jump in over her head. Sass had been with us for less than a week – and he'd come as a ten-week-old kitten – when there was a squeak of the heavy hinges and he came squirming triumphantly through.

His breeder was right about his being exceptional. This capacity of his for retrieving things, for instance... Up on the hill one afternoon, to my amazement, he picked up a fir-cone, brought it to me and put it down – and, when I threw it for him and it fell among a scattering of other cones, he chased it, searched it out by its scent, and brought the same one back. I encouraged him every afternoon after that by throwing pine-cones for him... further and further, till he'd come racing back with them right from the bottom of the hill, then lay them at my feet and sit down, bat ears at expectant angles, waiting for me to throw them for him again.

Fred Ferry spotted us at this in next to no time, of course, and went off to tell the tale round the village. Father Adams was watching from the lane the next time we came down off the hill. Sass, I should have mentioned, always brings his pine-cone back with him, trotting through the gate with it sticking out of his mouth and putting it down on the lawn.

'Well, if th'old liar weren't right for once,' said Father Adams. 'I wouldn't have believed it if I hadn't seen it for meself...' And off *he* went with an addendum to Fred's story. No wonder people think we are queer.

As they no doubt do when they see us with the cats on 20-foot leads... in the morning before breakfast, or when it is getting dusk. Never again will we take a chance with them... which has led to another complication. Sass the Exceptional has proved to be a tremendous jumper. He simply delights in leaping over things, which looks remarkable enough when he does it off his lead... over the wheelbarrow or a pile of bricks, for instance; or me, if I'm bending on the lawn. But when they are on their leads going into the orchard, and Shebalu demurely mounts the bar across the entrance and steps down the other side – and then Sass, lead and all, clears the whole thing high in the air like a grasshopper... no wonder people who see it look at us rather askance.

Not that we worry. At least we know they are safe, and gradually things have returned to normal. Charles is busy with his fruit trees and his painting. I go riding on Mio... I have learned to jump on him almost as well as Sass. The Bannetts have got their goat who, when they are away, quite often comes to stay with us.

'Thass all theest needed,' says Father Adams every time he sees her on our lawn. She and Sass heads down at one another, Shebalu looking primly on. Annabel bellowing down from the hillside about making a Fuss about Other People's rotten Goats. That is what we needed indeed, though there are some things we shall never forget. Nowadays, when we holiday in England, Sass and Shebalu come with us. They have seen the sea, and walked on a beach. Sass has even been in a boat. It is a long way from Canada to Cornwall... But that is another story.

www.summersdale.com